Paddington Boy

Paddington Boy

Arthur Barrett

ISIS
LARGE PRINT
Oxford

First published in Great Britain 2004
by
Bound Biographies Limited

Published in Large Print 2005 by ISIS Publishing Ltd,
7 Centremead, Osney Mead, Oxford OX2 0ES
by arrangement with the author

British Library Cataloguing in Publication Data
Barrett, Arthur
    Paddington boy. – Large print ed.
    (Isis reminiscence series)
    1. Barrett, Arthur
    2. Large type books
    3. London (England) – Biography
    4. Great Britain – Social life and customs – 20th
    century
    I. Title
    942.1'082'092

ISBN 0–7531–9308–6 (hb)
ISBN 0–7531–9309–4 (pb)

Printed and bound by Antony Rowe, Chippenham

Dedication

To my wife, Joan for her endless patience and to my daughters Pamela and Christine for their continued enthusiasm amid my swings of euphoria and despair. And to my new computer by whose grace I was allowed to finish without the sporadic interruption of the one I had before.

Contents

Acknowledgements

To the City of Westminster Archive Centre for introducing me to the fascinating world of Archives and in particular to the publication "Paddington" by Brian Girling to whom I am indebted for his permission to reproduce the photographs of "the place where I was born".

To the BT Archives for their details of the Strowger System and photographs of the Paddington Telephone Exchange for which I am pleased to acknowledge their courteous consent to inclusion in this book.

To the BBC Information and Archives for information relating to Messrs Dobson & Young and for supplying me with details of Radio programmes broadcast during the war years.

To the London Newspaper Group for their enthusiastic article in the Paddington Newspaper which led directly to the renewal of acquaintance with a former classmate who lived in the same street as myself.

To the Photographic Archive of the Imperial War Museum for their kind permission in reproducing photographs of war damage in the West End of London.

I acknowledge the courtesy and kindness that I was shown by each one in making my task a little easier.

My apologies if I have excluded any other contributor and an assurance it is unintentional and can be rectified.

Preface

Tom and Kathy were fellow residents of the retirement complex in which we both lived. Tom was born and bred in Tottenham in North London. A Territorial before the war he followed in his father's footsteps and began his soldiering in the Middlesex Regiment.

Keen on football he supported Tottenham Hotspur Football Club and was a true "Tottenham Boy".

I was born in Paddington in West London. My father was in the Middlesex Regiment during the First World War but I chose the Royal Navy.

I supported Queens Park Rangers and I was a "Paddington Boy".

Inevitably when we met our conversation invariably revolved around the game of football, that is when we were not putting the world aright.

When Tom died his wife, Kathy, gave me a book that Tom had compiled from letters he had received from his family during the bombing of London and she urged me to follow his example and write a book of my experiences of the War. If I ever had any inclination to write an autobiography this must have acted as a catalyst because "Paddington Boy" is the result.

You, my dear reader, may now picture me in my upper garret, crouched over my desk, my only companions a flickering candle and my own shadow on the wall behind me. The only sound, that of my pen as it scratches across the paper as I sit, my shawl around my shoulders in an effort to keep out the howling wind while I reach into the very depths of my memory as I search for inspiration. Or you may choose to see me comfortably at ease in a centrally heated home sitting at my aged computer that, with a challenging temperament, occasionally informs me that I have committed an illegal operation and will be closed down, or battling with a printer that decides it will only perform on Mondays, Wednesdays or Fridays and then only if there is an "R" in the month. So I renew both of them, and update my keyboard for good measure, only to find out that it is so sensitive that to my touch it produces three "a's" and two "d's" when I type the word minimum. I am tempted to liken my efforts to rowing across the Atlantic in a force nine gale, but that would be a gross exaggeration and what you now see is the result of many happy hours tinged with a soupcon of patience — not bad for an eighty year old is it? I recommend it but with a warning — it is an exercise that penetrated the very depths of nostalgia and it may be advisable to have a tissue handy to wipe away the occasional tear that might be activated in the process.

In the Beginning

'I remember, I remember the place where I was born.'
Thomas Hood (1799–1845)

I suppose the hardest part of writing a book is just getting started. One hears of the prolific author who can credit dozens of volumes to his name or the individual prompted by some "road to Damascus" revelation that causes them to suddenly leap out of bed and give rise to yet another epic tome. Me? I just simply want to tell you about my life as a Paddington Boy!

I emerged into this world, so I am told, on 28th August 1923 at about 5 o'clock in the afternoon in the Maida Hill district of Paddington, West London. That information should satisfy the budding astrologer who will discover that I was born with the Sun in Virgo and with Capricorn rising, which is reputed to carry the blueprint upon which my future existence is revealed. At this stage I was just satisfied to be born, but if I had then known what the next eighty odd years would be like I might have asked for a postponement — but I did not and so I had to get on with it.

I arrived at 71, Portnall Road, son of Stephen William and Lily Louise, and youngest brother of three sisters and another boy ... in fact, a very young brother since my eldest sister was sixteen years my senior and my brother twelve years, which meant our relationship was on a very adult basis from the start. I had no young playmates at home and if this deprivation had any effect on me I have never identified it, so it became a matter of not missing what I never had.

My father was a worker on the railway at Paddington and my mother had the fulltime occupation of looking after us all, which established the security and ideal environment that is seen to be sometimes lacking in this twenty-first century civilisation.

"Seventy-one", as our home became affectionately known for the rest of our days, was a large Victorian house, one of a number of terraced properties that extended the length of the road from Harrow Road to Shirland Road on its route to Kilburn Lane beyond. It comprised a semi-basement with a floor above and another above that, and entry to our living quarters in the basement was by steps down while the upper floors were served by a flight up to what was the main entrance. The basement contained a front room that served as my sisters' bedroom, which looked out into a small area surrounded by a privet hedge, a kitchen and beyond that a stone-floored scullery in which was the copper, a mangle, an ancient sink, and a door leading to a stone yard and a walled suburban garden. It became one of my jobs to whitewash the wall each year.

Cooking was achieved by a kitchen range with oven and, alongside, a small tank that provided a limited amount of hot rust-coloured water. It was to become my job to "black lead" the kitchen range and to chop the wood that was stored underneath. A system of dampers enabled the temperature of the oven to be controlled, and Mum had the knack of being able, just by feeling the oven handle, of ascertaining the correct heat required for any particular item of cooking. On the top of the stove stood the saucepans and a kettle, which always seemed to be on the point of boiling and ready to make a cup of tea. It was frequently necessary to clear the stove of accumulated soot, a dirty job for which we had the appropriate tools — a task which I later enjoyed doing just for the pleasure of seeing the black mass emerge and which generally ended up being deposited in the garden . . . we never had any trouble with slugs or snails. The basement was served by a long passage running from the downstairs front door and was our means of entry at all times. Apart from my sleeping quarters upstairs this was the extent of my world.

The upper parts of the house, reached by a wooden staircase, I seldom saw and rarely ventured into, being partly occupied by a tenant of my parents. Their access was from the road, via the front steps, and a glass-fronted door bearing the number of the house and the letterbox. It was common practice that these steps were kept white by the occasional application of water and hearthstone, which was possibly why we rarely used this means of entry. It was never a job I enjoyed doing.

My recollections of life did not occur until I started school soon after my third birthday, and I still have some vague memories of going to school with a handkerchief pinned to my front. I was not alone in this attire, and dealing with runny noses was but one of the chores undertaken by the teacher. I remember, too, playing with sand in a big wooden box and having the usual accompaniment of simple toys. In the afternoon we slept and our accommodation for this consisted of a hammock-like contraption slung between the four legs of a small upturned table. One vivid memory, which is uppermost in my mind even today, is that someone always wet the bed and I recall seeing the tell-tale damp patch. Needless, to say I never remember being among the culprits.

The school was situated a short walk up the Harrow Road, but crossing a main road which in those days featured horse-drawn vehicles and tramcars along the middle. This was, of course, before the days of school crossing personnel affectionately known as "lollipop ladies" and our safety was entrusted to a member of the local constabulary. The building consisted of a large two-storey structure, the ground floor containing the Infant school and the remainder devoted to Senior accommodation. My brother had attended both and I was to follow in due course.

Recollection of my Senior School occupation relates to an injury suffered by the policeman who chaperoned us across the road and we were each encouraged to write a letter for delivery to his hospital bed. Another recollection concerns the local fire brigade whose engine, accompanied by the loud ringing of its bell, announced its progress along the road at which all the class, with one exception, rushed to the window to view the exciting phenomenon. Little me, sporting an imaginary halo, remained firmly in my seat for fear of being severely reprimanded!

Of the remainder of my sojourn at the Moberley School I have little recollection, except for the fact that at morning assembly in the Senior School we always seemed to sing one of three hymns. One still eludes, but the remaining two were: There is a Green Hill Far Away and Hushed was the Evening Hymn. Even today, hearing either hymn triggers instant recall and also my concern as to why a green hill should have a city wall, which enigma lasted well into my later years. I also remember that the school had a very large playground in which was situated the caretaker's house where I, with a selected few, was invited to play after school. This sometimes featured a helping of homemade ice-cream, and for this reason alone such friendship was to be treasured. I did, however, blot my copybook in some way and was thereafter and forever banned.

Moberley School was limited to the under-elevens, and the time came when my focus was directed to leaving infancy behind and joining the bigger boys elsewhere. This was the time, my parents informed me, that my education came first and this priority was to act against some of my ambitions that lay elsewhere. What followed had a recognisable influence on the level of my education and my subsequent venture into the world of the working man, but in the meantime I was still "little Arthur" and beginning to learn about family life.

For as long as I can remember everything revolved around the one room: decisions were made, people were entertained and the inner man was sustained in the kitchen. The front room upstairs was more comfortably furnished, but in keeping with the practice of the time was strictly reserved for those special occasions which justified removing the dust sheets from the furniture and giving the aspidistra a refreshing polish. In the meantime the kitchen table was the focal point. It was a large white, sturdily-built wooden affair upon which food was prepared and eaten, and around which the Sunday lunch saw the whole family gathered together for the only time in the week.

The menu at meal times followed the same pattern each week. Sunday would see the emergence of the weekly joint, invariably beef but occasionally lamb, which Mum would have bought on Saturday by waiting until the butcher was ready to close when he would offer choice cuts of meat at reduced prices. This was a common practice of many of the traders along the Harrow Road and housewives were not slow in taking advantage of saving a few coppers. Monday, being wash-day, produced a simple and easy meal consisting of a cold slice or two of the Sunday joint with left-over vegetables being fried — a favourite known as "bubble and squeak". Tuesday saw a little more of the Sunday joint, which was finally dispatched in the form of mince and served on Wednesday. We were fortunate to be able to have meat most days, and I was sometimes sent to the butchers with a request for "best end of neck" or some stewing steak. Fish was invariably limited to

Friday, not for any religious reason, but because we had a cold fish shop at the end of the road, where I would watch the live eels wriggling in a box and sometimes escaping across the pavement in the direction of the nearest drain. Saturday completed the weekly round with a serving of liver and bacon or sausage and mashed potatoes, generally referred to as "bangers and mash".

The table was regularly scrubbed to accommodate for the making of pastry and other cooking activities, and when not in use was covered with a large chenille tablecloth, matching the decoration that surrounded the mantelpiece. Underneath was a capacious space into which I retreated and was content to play with my toys and so avoid the toing and froing of six pairs of feet when the whole family was assembled.

Sitting accommodation comprised sufficient chairs strategically placed between table and wall, necessitating a small mountaineering exercise to reach the farthest ones. Mum and Dad had their own chairs, small carver-type ones that adorned either side of the kitchen range; visitors and the rest of the family resorted to wherever they could find a space. Comfortable it surprisingly was, and with the kitchen range in use all the year it was never cold — and if it got overheated there was always the large window, which opened upon the back yard.

Toilet facilities, in keeping with the day and age, can adequately be described as "outside in the yard", a small, cold, dark but temporary abode which, in the winter, one approached with foreboding and a lighted candle.

The stone-floored scullery down the passage provided the means of washing crockery, pots and pans, and, not least, ourselves, and on wash days was filled with steam during the washing of clothes. It also supplied the cold water from the mains to enable the foregoing to be accomplished. The scullery became the focus of activity from early on Monday morning when Mum (or Dad, if he was on an early turn at work) would be up early to light the copper fire that had been prepared with wood the night before. I would awake to the sound of scrubbing and a room full of steam. Mum would open the window to watch the steam as it went out — if it rose up it would signify a good drying day while any other result generally confined the washing to drying indoors. This was when the mangle was an essential piece of equipment and I would, if I had time before school, help Mum by turning the handle and watching the water squeeze out into a bucket strategically placed underneath.

As winter approached I would be the subject of certain forms of medication traditionally directed at the younger generation to ward off the ills that might otherwise befall us. No doubt my brother and sisters had also been subject to this legacy of the Victorian age. The box of "Carter's Little Liver Pills" would be produced and one or two administered, not because I needed them, but as an insurance against a variety of ills. A visit to the lavatory would invoke the enquiry "have you been?" A negative reply would see the emergence of a choice of remedies, and I had the pick of a supply of castor oil, senna pods, or a yellowish-green mixture that resulted when liquorice powder was mixed with a small amount of milk. Whatever was chosen I sought my own time to demolish one or other of the horrible concoctions.

Any complaint of a muscular ache could easily be dismissed as "growing pains" or see an application of a liniment in the form of White Horse Oil, which Dad had made up for him by a colleague at work. A good rub left me with an odour appropriate to a stable after a visit from the veterinary doctor, but my brother found it useful after a long cycle ride, as I did some time later. To complete the medicine chest we always kept a bottle of smelling salts that Dad made up from time to time with the aid of a bottle of ammonia. I was kept well away from the latter as it had a pungent smell that could be dangerous to the uninitiated, but it was all part of the Victorian addiction to one's health that prevailed at this time.

Of my sisters Doris, hereafter and forever known as Dorrie, might be described, not unkindly, as the eldest and shop steward of the siblings to follow, a position she would naturally have acquired at the beginning of the First World War because she was given responsibility to help Mum to bring up the remaining three young children while Dad was in the Army. This acquired authority she retained to the end of her days, and it was always accepted that she was a mine of information on all things relating to the Barrett clan. I miss her expertise today and regret, perhaps, that I did not start this venture years ago — I am sure she could have filled in a good few holes in my recollection as she played an important part in my life at 71 Portnall Road.

Two girls followed, Hilda and Elsie, and the arrival of my brother George in 1911 brought an end to the family until my arrival 12 years later from luck, design or accident. Whatever the reason, I can only hope that, with hindsight, I was worth it.

Fortunately all, with the exception of my mother, were gainfully employed. I say "gainfully" because this must have been about the time of the General Strike in 1926, but I was not sensitive to any atmosphere nor understanding of what conversation there was during a period that was known as the Depression. However, in our house there were plenty of comings and goings and most, if not all, were over my little head — quite literally so since I preferred the space underneath the table to play. This is not to say that I never had contact with my brother and sisters. It was invariably one of my sisters who executed my nightly wash and preparation for bed. I remember that this involved a large bowl on the table and my standing in it being washed top to toe, followed by being carried up to the double bed I shared with my brother, until the coming of hostilities in 1939 separated us.

A weekly event involved the large galvanised bath that hung on the outside wall in the yard, which was brought in and placed in front of the kitchen range fire. Whether the whole family was subjected to this ritual I never found out, but I vaguely recall the scullery being called into service, with heating provided by oil stove.

At that time there were such places as bathhouses where one could take the weekly ablution for the cost of a few pence and they were, I later discovered, well supported.

I was growing up but still encased in a little world of my own. I was "Little Arthur" which rather emphasised the gap that existed between myself and the rest of the family, a gap I never really breeched. I lived in a world of my own — I had my books and my toys, and I played indoors and in the garden whilst I steadily and imperceptibly passed from the infant to the young child. I remember very little of it, and the fact that at some time I was able to read showed that I had received some instruction, although I do not recall the experience of any of the three "R's". I remember I had a number of books which included a large red volume of fairy tales, and I became well acquainted with Hansel and Gretel, Rumpelstiltskin and Snow White to name but a few of the stories which kept me enraptured. I also had a book of Aesop's Fables, which I do remember impressed me with the Philosophy contained in the simple stories. I do hope the book is still available to the younger generation — it should be. To complete a trio, I had a book detailing the peoples of the world in pictures, which must rate as my first introduction to racial distinction ... I hope it was responsible for the tolerance I have today. That such books were available was due to the practice of certain newspapers, and I remember the *Daily Herald* in particular featured coupons that could be cut out and exchanged for a variety of quality books at reasonable cost. They made excellent Christmas presents and I must have benefited by this means.

At this time Radio was in the development stage and children had more time to read and play and develop without any influence from this quarter; times have moved on since then and programmes dedicated to the learning process form no part in a young person's life. My eldest sister had a very fine copy of *Alice in Wonderland*, an impressive volume with gold lettering and gold edges to the pages. I was not allowed to touch, but my sister read a passage from it to me each evening. Later I was given permission, and read the story again to my great pleasure.

I had a fair share of toys as well. Like most boys I had a train set which grew as each Christmas passed, until it reached such proportion that I had to retire to my bedroom floor to give it enough room. I had a Bagatelle game, and since I had no young brothers or sisters to share it with I invented games I could play on my own. On the rare occasions that I was allowed young friends in to play, we were relegated to the garden and amused ourselves there. And so I gradually grew up and began to develop relationships with the rest of the family — seeing my elders as individual personalities and not people who came into my life at teatime and left before I had breakfast the next day.

I was emerging from the stage of "being seen but not heard", but not sufficiently so that I was involved in any family discussion. Nevertheless, I was developing my own personality and at the same time creating "pen pictures" of those around me that were to last for the rest of my life.

DAD

A gentle man, country-born in a little village in Oxfordshire, Dad had a kind, simple nature dedicated to the service of others. He served in the Middlesex Regiment during the 1914–18 war, and was one of the 'contemptible little army,' an expression of the German Kaiser in describing the British Expeditionary Force that had landed in France in 1914. Dad survived the war and returned to his job with the Great Western Railway at Paddington Station.

The railway was an important source of employment to the people of Paddington — it could represent a job for life, with rewards for long service, and was considered the ultimate in security for the working classes. Dad was a member of the Great Western Branch of the St John Ambulance Association, and I have his original first aid certificate in which he qualified as a first aider, awarded to him by the Association in 1907. He was an instructor in First Aid for many years, and my brother qualified under his tuition and followed him in his dedication to ambulance work.

In the railway community at Paddington, Dad was known as "Doc" to his ambulance colleagues. He received a commendation for saving the life of a colleague knocked down on the railway line, and who suffered a serious leg injury in the accident. For his long and dedicated service to the St John Ambulance Brigade, Dad was made a Serving Brother of the Order of St John of Jerusalem, an honour later awarded to my brother who also had a record of long service in the Brigade. I regret I was not to follow either of them, as I would have liked, as my parents felt that my education came first and I was not encouraged to join any boys' organisations. Dad finally retired after serving as the First Aid Co-ordinator for the A.R.P. (Air Raid Precautions) office at Paddington, set up during the war years, and with a credit of over 40 years service to the community and the G.W.R. In his last years, Dad was in poor health and I used to collect his pension each week from the local railway station — a ten-shilling note (50p).

To my young mind, Dad was synonymous with the railway and with Paddington Station. He was a travelling ticket collector on long distant trains, and during the school holidays I sometimes accompanied him on his journeys ... a real treat for me as it invariably included dinner on the train and ice cream for afters. Once I was old enough to be let out on my own, I frequently met him "off the train", just for the thrill of carrying his signal lantern along the platform. On a Sunday I would take a penny bus ride to Paddington Station and wait near the arrival board until Dad's train was signalled, meanwhile listening to the G.W.R. Band that regularly played upon the forecourt, which was known as "The Lawn", but there was not a blade of grass in sight. The train was rarely late, even from as far as the West Country, and I detected an element of pride that was a feature then of those employed by the G.W.R. — the "Greatest Way Round" to its critics but to our family it was "God's Wonderful Railway". I had great affection for Dad and hope I may have inherited just some of his virtues . . . I can only strive to do so as I could not wish for a better example.

MUM

Mum, who hailed from Notting Hill Gate, West London, was a matriarchal figure, making the important decisions and controlling all the finances. She was self-assured and a perfect foil for the gentleness of Dad who was content to leave her in sole charge. At the time of the outbreak of World War I, Mum had four young children to bring up in the absence of my father overseas. From what I was told by my eldest sister, Mum lost no time in co-opting her to assist in looking after the household. I do not think that anybody claimed that they were able to "get round Mum", and she encouraged us each in turn to take an active part in household chores. It was no accident that I was eventually able to peel potatoes, chop wood and clean both inside and outside of the windows, and I was also often given the job of mixing the mustard or making mint sauce to accompany the Sunday dinner. In short, Mum was a methodical, hard-working housewife and mother although at times . . . she led by example.

15

On occasions Mum was forced to take to her bed for the day for what I believe must have been migraine attacks, but she had trained her children well and the rest of the family were well prepared to cope.

It was Mum who largely directed my education and she would let nothing get in the way. My brother and sisters were not able to get a great education — I do not think one was available to those in our working class strata. Because she may have felt some responsibility for this, Mum was equally determined that I should not follow suit and so I was encouraged at every opportunity, and it was through her dedication that I was able to get employment in the General Post Office Engineering Department and train as a telephone engineer.

Mum went blind in later life and the family that she had so carefully created rallied round and took much of the weight off Dad's shoulders. She displayed great courage during this disability, and my recollection of this time still leaves me noticeably moved.

I could not have deserved such devoted and caring parents; they formed the cornerstone, and taught us the value of maintaining the family relationship that should be carried on and practised by each succeeding generation.

DORIS

Although christened Doris, I do not think she was ever so called. To the family she was Dorrie, and I shall continue to maintain this tradition . . . I should feel awkward doing otherwise. Dorrie was the eldest of the three girls and the one of whom I have the clearest recollection, and who was to have the greatest influence on me in later years. A tall and upright figure, I remember Dorrie as something of a matriarch, even after my formative years — she may have developed this when she was "put in charge" of the rest of the young family during the First World War.

Dorrie was a pianist and singer who inclined towards classical music, and my earliest recollection is of the strains of piano practice emanating from the front room above, a cold room without winter heating. Dorrie often told me of the times she was made to practise, despite the fact that she could barely feel the notes. On one occasion, and just within my memory, she had to practise whilst the coffin of our recently deceased Uncle George stood betrestled behind her. But it had its rewards. Dorrie became an accomplished performer with a fine contralto voice, and with the aid of an old wind-up gramophone she introduced me to the likes of Elgar, Ketelbey and others, and young as I was I remember it had a certain appeal. I had one particular favourite — Praeludium by Jarnefelt, which because of its rhythm I nicknamed the "plink-plonk" song and requested it many times. Appreciation did not extend to the rest of the family, and my father referred to it as "pot music"; my other sisters were more interested in the popular tunes of the day.

Association with Dorrie was to be interrupted when, having married, she and her husband Harold Gill left for India where he worked as an accountant in

Calcutta. For the next few years she sent me many photographs of Indian life, with an appropriate commentary, and I still have these today — of course these were the days of the Raj and the English presence was to be terminated later. The round of tennis parties and other social activities enabled her to hone her hostess qualities even further, which we found to our benefit some years later.

Before her marriage, Dorrie was an operator at the "Trunks" telephone exchange which was the centre for all outgoing and incoming international telephone communications. This was a prelude to a family association with the Post Office, which spanned many years.

Dorrie was keen on activities that promoted an interest in health and fitness, a popular fashion followed by the young men and women of the day. She regularly took part in hiking excursions, principally at weekends when a short journey into the country terminated in exploration of the English countryside — those who indulged became the pioneers of the organised ramblers' associations of today.

Dorrie returned to England in 1937 with a young son, Francis, but by then I had moved on from the fledgling stage and was learning to spread my own wings and develop separate interests. I was to resume my close contact with Dorrie some time in later life when I found we shared the same philosophy in seeking the causes and nature of things relating to a material and spiritual existence.

HILDA

The second of the girls, Hilda quite naturally acquired the name of "Sis", which remained her title for the rest of her life. She could have reasonably been described as a "thoroughly modern Millie", as she was a keen and competent dancer, well versed in the latest trends in fashion and music. I remember Sis trying to teach my other sisters the steps of the "Black Bottom", or the "Charleston", which in our small kitchen was difficult to say the least. I might add that Dad was not amused, but I admired his patience!

Sis, like most girls, liked to apply the cosmetic arts and I can vividly recall the sight of my three sisters vying for a place in front of the large kitchen mirror. Poor Dad, once again! It would be wrong to suggest that all was forever calm and serene in the female camp, and the occasional argument ensued with one or other of them seeking the support of Dad in furthering their particular cause. It has been known for the odd hairbrush to become airborne in their bedroom next door to the kitchen, with Dad once again being involuntarily involved. His patience amazingly remained intact.

Sis was also an accomplished needlewoman, and her latest creation could usually be seen hanging on the bedroom wall. I do believe she made more dresses than she actually wore, with someone else generally benefiting from her labours.

Sis was also a Telephone Operator and, as I recall, was employed at the Cunningham and Abercorn

19

exchanges. She subsequently married a Telephone Engineer and left the family home. Close contact with Sis ceased, although I did occasionally stay with her during the school holidays. The association with the Post Office Telephone Service was to be further perpetuated when I, much later, became a Telephone Engineer, but I must not pre-empt this event here.

ELSIE

Elsie was the last of the distaff branch of the family, and the one who I never really got to know or can remember much about, except for the fact that she was always the manager of Messrs Eastmans, a dry cleaners shop in Oxford Street, central London. She never featured greatly in my life, but I do remember that she was courted by, and subsequently married, the "boy next door" . . . or to be more precise the boy over the road, Charlie Waller. Mr & Mrs Waller lived at No. 54; Mr Waller was a painter and decorator and often did work for my Dad. Charlie Waller often visited our house, and I recall that his approach down the area steps was heralded by loud singing which continued down the passage as his voice was raised in a rendering of Only a Rose, a popular song of the day, much to the chagrin of my somewhat staid Victorian parents. Charlie was merely giving voice to my sister's second name — she was christened Elsie Rose.

Elsie and Charlie eventually married and set up home on one of the many estates being built around London. This was the beginning of the 1930s urban sprawl in the environs of London, when houses were being offered for low deposit with monthly instalments of the balance — I believe their house cost £500. Elsie and Sis lived in adjoining streets, and I had to take good care when I visited that I shared my attention equally between the two for fear of offending one or the other.

I remember an occasion when Charlie decided to repaint his house in the colour of peaches and cream, which my parents considered a reactionary break from tradition. Personally I liked it, although it might have shattered the popular conception of decorating style — but this was the era of change and Charlie was in the forefront of it.

Sad to say, the family was depleted when Elsie died in her middle 40s, leaving three young children, Adrian, Doreen ("Dorphie") and Barry, for her husband to bring up. She was sadly missed at our family gatherings, but we have always kept in touch with her family.

GEORGE

My first recollection of my brother is sharing a large brass bedstead in the small back room on the first floor. It was, I believe, originally meant to be a kitchen because it was provided with a kitchen range clearly intended for cooking but had never been used for this purpose. In front stood a large wooden box and upon which, at Christmas time, I used to lay a large pillow in the hope that it would be filled overnight. To my disappointment it was not and I remember I nearly burst into tears on one occasion until I found my presents lying on the floor behind me.

Although we shared the same sleeping accommodation I saw very little of George during the week as he left early in the mornings and came back after I was asleep, although I sometimes lay awake waiting for him to come home — it was a big bed and I wanted the feeling of security his presence brought.

My only other recollection at this time is that he worked as a packer of china and glass for William Whiteley & Co, a large departmental store, which I believe still has a shop in Queensway, Bayswater today. This proved to be a useful occupation, because when Dorrie went to India after her marriage he undertook the packing of all her china and glass. I had a hand in this as I made successive visits to a local carpenter's yard to collect supplies of wood shavings and sawdust that were freely given, although I sometimes had to sweep them up myself. It should be recorded that George's efforts were wholly successful and there were no breakages.

George was a keen cyclist and one had to manoeuvre past his cycle in the downstairs passage, something which occasionally produced mutterings of discontent, especially from the ladies who feared damage to their legs or, more especially, their stockings. He became a member of the Cyclist's Touring Club (which then had its headquarters close to Paddington Station) and spent many weekends with the local cycling group. Many of his holidays were enjoyed touring, using the facilities of the Youth Hostel Association that provided cheap and friendly accommodation for walkers and cyclists alike, and regular postcards kept us in touch with his progress. Postcards cost a penny to send and would be delivered the next day.

It was not long, as I remember, before a tandem appeared in the passage and I once rode on the back seat on a trip to an aunt who lived in Buckinghamshire — much to Mum's consternation. I enjoyed the experience, which may have been the catalyst that caused me take up the sport in my later years. The rear seat was thereafter occupied by a young lady who ultimately became George's wife.

But my most vivid memories relate to the family association with the St John's Ambulance Brigade. Dad was already an established member of the Paddington Railway branch, and when my brother joined the Wembley branch it signalled the start of much lighthearted competition between them, especially in the direction of smartness of turnout. There was frequent activity of polishing of belts and whitening of cap bands, and although Dad trusted me in this respect, my brother never took up my offers. He was a dedicated member of the Brigade and took every available course to improve his knowledge. To this end he joined the Royal Naval Sickberth Reserve, membership of which was extended to St John's Ambulance personnel and which necessitated annual attendance for hospital training at various Royal Naval Establishments. It was on one of these occasions that

23

an incident occurred that involved both George and my father.

George travelled to Plymouth for his annual training on the train on which Dad was Ticket Collector. At Totnes station the train began to move before loading was complete and Dad hurried to apply the emergency brake in the Guard's Van, which he successfully managed to do only to collapse shortly afterwards. George and his ambulance colleagues were soon on the scene and Dad was quickly taken to a hospital in Plymouth where he made a complete recovery.

Soon after, the clouds of war gathered and my brother and I were separated when he was called to the Sick Berth Branch of the Royal Navy. During his war service he gained experience in every hospital discipline, with the possible exception of maternity, and he could have taken a senior position in any hospital ward but the financial rewards were insufficient to maintain a young family. He continued his voluntary work after the war and followed my father in becoming a Serving Brother of the Order of St John, an award justly earned. He set me an example I could not emulate.

Out of Doors

My principal play areas were confined to the kitchen and our small suburban garden. Although small, the garden was well maintained with plants and afforded me all the room I needed to give my imagination full rein in my games. I played on my own and it was only much later that I had friends in to play.

Everyday we went shopping — that is, Mum took me along the Harrow Road, which was our principal shopping area. This entailed a short walk up the road, clutching Mum's hand, and invariably stopping along the way as we would surely meet one of our neighbours. This meant an exchange of news, views and opinions in the form of a sharing of local intelligence. I remember this always seemed to take a long time, and I would stand somewhat impatiently, occasionally tugging at my mother's hand in an attempt to get her to continue our expedition. This was not an uncommon feature of our neighbourhood and it was quite usual to see groups of apronclad ladies, generally with their hair in curlers or hidden by a neatly arranged scarf, standing at the front gates in earnest conversation. In this way the fortunes or misfortunes of members of the community were revealed, and where help was needed there was always a helping hand to be had. Eventually we would arrive at our intended destination.

Harrow Road extended from the Edgware Road through our part of Paddington and on to Wembley and beyond. The shopping centre part ran from the Prince of Wales for some three hundred yards. The "Prince of Wales" was the intersection of a number of roads, a communal meeting place with the inevitable pub that gave the small area its name. It featured the central figure of a policeman, complete with white armbands, standing in the centre directing the traffic.

We were well equipped with shops, and I could count three bakers, four grocers and three greengrocers, not including the costermonger's stall at the top of Portnall Road. F.W. Woolworth advertised that it sold "nothing over sixpence", and in my young recollection it never did. Across the road was a penny bazaar, which rumour had it was a forerunner of Marks and Spencer. The ladies were well catered for at a large haberdashery where one could buy clothing material and curtaining from a penny three-farthings a yard, while next door stood the ironmongers which sold most requirements from little boxes behind its long counter, and where a friendly assistant would willingly advise on one's dilemmas. Butchers were well in evidence, and a little later in life I was detailed to 'ask for a pound of scrag end,' or 'have you got a bone to spare?' This was after I had visited one of the three bakeries to enquire whether they had any of yesterday's bread or cakes left — if so I was well rewarded with a bagful for sixpence. I also got a rosy apple for one halfpenny from the greengrocer on my way to school.

By now I was allowed "out of doors"; I frequently went to play with the local children and so began a kaleidoscope of memories. Our playground was the street and sometimes somebody else's, but there was plenty of room and compared with today it was relatively safe. We were seldom troubled by passing traffic and any such would merely serve as a short interruption of our games. Mostly it was horse-drawn, of which the coalman selling his wares at two and sixpence a hundredweight was most common, followed by a horse-drawn dustcart once a week. Motorcars were a rarity in our street, and any that did stop at one of the houses generally raised enough boyish interest to attract a crowd around it.

We played all the seasonal games and were all boys together — I do not recollect any female participation in our activities. Of course there were young girls in our community, but girls couldn't hold a bat, kick a football or throw straight, so I suppose we were displaying an early tendency to male chauvinism . . . unintended of course! We played football across the whole width of the road, and cricket against any one of a number of lampposts the bottom of which closely resembled the size and shape of a set of stumps. A tennis ball served for all our games, and with the hard surface of the pavement and the speed of the ball we honed our skills and imagined that we were one of the leading cricketers of the day. Looking back I would venture to suggest that we created our own cricketing academy and that many of the fine exponents of the game at that time had done likewise. Such was our skill that, despite being surrounded as we were by so many large windows, I do not remember any coming to grief on our account. We had no other arena in which to play — the only park facility was a good walk away and games were not permitted.

Another use for the lamppost was for the game we knew as "Jimmy Knacker", one, it appears, which had a universal appeal. *Children's Games in Street and Playground* (Oxford University Press) by Iona and Peter Opie, 1969, gives some of the names attributed worldwide: in Tyneside it is "Mountykitty", "Pomperino" in Cornwall, and in Italy it goes under the name of "Il Cavallo Lungo" (the long horse), which best describes its formation.

One boy stood with his back to the lamppost, whilst the next one bent down and clutched him around the waist, followed by the rest of the team who, similarly bent, each held on to the boy in front, until you had an assembly of bent backs. The object of the other team was to run and leap, one by one, along the line of backs getting as far forward as possible, the object being to cause the collapse of the line. The chant then rang out:

> Hi Jimmy Knacker,
> One two three.
> Hi Jimmy Knacker,
> Gone for his tea!

If the line survived, the positions were reversed for the next attempt.

Not all our games were so energetic, and many had an annual cycle, coming round at the same time each year. When the horse chestnuts began to fall in the local park we would quickly gather as many as we could hoping that amongst them we would find one to beat all-comers. I must admit that we tried various methods to achieve this, not least baking in the oven or steeping in vinegar — we had no regulating body to ensure fair play.

Marbles, some beautifully coloured, featured regularly each year, and we retrieved the previous year's supply from the back of a cupboard ready to give battle. We would play by rolling our marbles along the gutter, skillfully avoiding the drains, and we measured the proximity of our marble to the next by the span of the thumb and little finger. Winner takes all.

Cigarette cards were the product of packets of cigarettes and were obtained from any smoker we might meet. They covered many subjects, some of which were extremely educational. They were used in barter and exchange, but collections in mint condition can nowadays command good prices at the right auction. Those surplus to requirements were used in a variety of games, one of which entailed "flicking" one card across the pavement in an attempt to partly or wholly cover that of your opponent. Success meant you acquired his card, adding it to your collection — thus the extent of the wealth of any boy was revealed by the size of his collection of marbles and cigarette cards. But fortunes were occasionally made and lost in a single afternoon's play.

My greatest thrill during the school holidays was to accompany Dad on one of his trips to Penzance. I would arrive at Paddington Station in order to meet Dad on the platform, and sometimes I would arrive early so that I could wander around the station and look at the engines on other platforms. My pride and joy lay in the "King" class, the most powerful of the locomotives used by the G.W.R., and my day would be complete if I saw the King George V because it had a golden bell on the front celebrating the Silver Jubilee of King George V and Queen Mary. The other "Hall" and "Castle" classes were well worth viewing and they all represented the might of the steam train era.

Dad's train would be classified as the 11 o'clock down to Penzance, and was appropriately named the "Cornishman", a name that was displayed along the tops of the coaches. I would wait to see the engine that was to pull the train coupled up, and if I was lucky I would be invited to stand on the footplate along with the engine driver and fireman for a short time before we left. At the appointed time Dad would blow his whistle, wave a green flag, and hop on the train as it moved slowly away, and we were off.

On the way down Dad would point out places of interest, among them the White Horse carved in the Wiltshire Downs and the Wellington Monument standing proud on the horizon. At Plymouth it was the practice to change the engine for a lighter one which better suited the track through Cornwall. We would soon be crossing the Royal Albert Bridge at Saltash, built by Isambard Brunel over the river Tamar, and opened in 1859. We would have lunch on the train, another treat because it provided a choice of ice cream for afters and the grandeur of sitting in the Dining Car to eat it.

When I saw St Michael's Mount out at sea I knew our arrival at Penzance was imminent, and in the evening Dad would take me around the town and to the quayside to see the Scillonian which took passengers to the Scilly Isles. We ended the day with fish and chips before retiring to our overnight accommodation. This was always with a retired engine driver and his wife, and I remember the memorabilia of the Great Western Railway that were displayed around the walls. There was a pride in the railway possessed by all who worked on it, and Dad was no exception.

Our return trip the next morning was a repeat of our journey down. I remember that we always arrived on time, and Dad always made a point of thanking the engine driver and his mate. It was a happy youngster who went to bed that night, and in the morning I would be back seeking my pleasure in the street.

When the cricket season arrived we would venture away from our usual haunts, taking sandwiches and a bottle of lemonade on our journey to Lord's cricket ground a bus ride away. Middlesex being our local county cricket team, we were naturally keen supporters and not the only youngsters watching our favourite players. I do not remember any trouble arising from our presence; we were engrossed in the game and religiously kept the score on the scorecards we had bought for a penny or two. If we had pennies to spare we would treat ourselves to sweets or an ice cream.

Our finances came from wherever we could create a source. Running errands for neighbours would always yield a halfpenny or a penny, and occasionally we became a little more adventurous — we would tour the shops in the Harrow Road, and especially the greengrocers, in the hope of being given unwanted wooden boxes. These would be taken home and a joint assault with a chopper reduced them to kindling wood, which we tied in bundles and hawked around the immediate neighbourhood. We were generous in the size of our wares, which met with an equal financial response that we shared amongst us. It provided enough for a short time, until we felt the need to repeat the exercise. As I remember, none of us had a regular allowance of pocket money.

Our summer activities would not be complete without the annual holiday, always, I seem to remember, taken at the end of August, and always to Great Yarmouth where we stayed in the same accommodation as the previous year. My memories revolve around sun, sea and sand, the Britannia and Wellington Piers, and standing in shelters away from the rain. I always seemed to get sunburnt, and thunderstorms came only at night — little else comes to mind in all the years we honoured the place with our presence.

The onset of the shorter days brought an end to our summer contentment, and we retreated indoors to retrieve the books we had put away in the spring. The "wireless" was to be our source of entertainment for the next few months. Our wireless, as it was then known — when it became a "radio" I have no idea — consisted of a large box with a sloping front and containing something called a "cat's whisker". On the front was a large circular dial that, when turned, would, after a series of howls and screeches, finally produce a sound that could be heard coming from the speaker alongside. This could be either talking or music, which meant we could settle down and listen . . . but not for long. Our neighbour would be similarly equipped, and the tuning of his wireless set resulted in more howls emanating from our speaker until he, in turn, had "tuned in" to the station.

The British Broadcasting Company provided the programmes, later becoming the British Broadcasting Corporation or BBC that we know today. Many of these sets were homemade, being based upon a simple circuit. They required an accumulator for low voltage supply, and a battery that provided a higher one. Both of these required frequent renewal, the accumulator more so, and I remember that I took ours to the shop at the top of the road and exchanged it for a fully charged replacement at least once a week. Thus we kept ourselves occupied during the long winter evenings that alternated between table games, reading and the wireless.

Saturday was a football day, and a few of us would catch the train to Shepherd's Bush and make the short walk to the ground of Queen's Park Rangers at Loftus

Road, then in the Third Division (South) of the football league. The Rangers were our local football heroes and we were avid supporters. Their fortunes have fluctuated since those days, but I am still an ardent follower of the present club. In the event that they were playing away, we would transfer our support temporarily to the Fulham club at Craven Cottage, a bus ride or a walk farther away, or take the trip to Stamford Bridge to watch Chelsea. Teams in those days generally included local talent developed from playing the game at school. In all this time I never remember violence breaking out; in fact the younger ones were helped to the front to get a better view and our parents never had cause to fear for our safety. The present state of sport in general is a sad reflection of those days and seems to lack the security we enjoyed.

School Days

According to my parents, I had now reached a level where my education was a serious business in that it was to place some restriction on my out-of-school activities. In spite of my requests, I was not allowed to become a Boy Scout or join any other youthful activity because it would, as they said, interfere with my education. I can now understand their point of view. I believe my brother and sisters may not have had the opportunities that were now open to me and my parents perhaps felt some measure of responsibility for this. I do know that my brother felt very keenly that he had been deprived and may have voiced his disappointment, so my parents were determined that there should be no repetition.

In any event I had a good education, although I was not to display any dynamism. My English teacher described my progress adequately when, upon reading one of my essays, he remarked, "Barrett — a good essay, but you always seem to just miss the boat". A fair comment, but at least I reaped the benefit that my brother and sisters were denied.

At some time I must have left the "big boys" at the Moberley School because I have a fleeting memory of attending another school in Droop Street, Queens Park, not far from where I lived. This must have been what was then described as a Junior School for it led, via a scholarship examination, to a choice of schools at senior level. I believe I must have taken this test, but I have no recollection of having done so, perhaps because it did not attract the publicity that similar examinations do today. In any event something led me to be involved in an interview with the Headmaster of the North Paddington Central School for Boys, which I remember attending with another boy.

During the course of the interview the other boy, in answer to a question by the Head, said that his mother wanted him to come and that he liked the school. In answer to the same question, I replied that I "wanted a better education" but from what source I got the inspiration for this remark I do not know; however, I was selected in preference to my fellow pupil.

The alternative to the Central, at which one learnt French and left at 16, was the "Senior School" which gave a more basic education and from which one left at 14 to face life in the outside world. Entry to a grammar school was strictly by application, followed by an examination of some kind and an interview — I, having applied, fell at the first fence . . . perhaps I had, once more, just missed the boat.

Preparations began for what was to be the last lap in the quest for knowledge. A school uniform and cap were mandatory and acquired by way of a local outfitter, the school having a supply of second-hand blazers for those parents who could not afford to buy new. Caps very rarely survived to become re-usable as they were occasionally snatched from one's head and used as temporary footballs. Thus was I introduced to a world of poverty that I had not realised existed, and I recognised a sort of stigma that attached to a boy wearing secondhand clothes, often referred to as "hand-me-downs". I had previously been confined to the small community around where I lived, but now I was to be introduced to boys from farther afield and from a different social stratum.

In particular I met boys from hitherto uncharted territory on the other side of the canal which ran alongside the Harrow Road. It was approached by crossing the "half-penny" steps into an area known as Kensal Town, which we in our childish way had avoided in the belief that it was a rough area containing all sorts of undesirables. How this myth arose, I do not know, but it was all part of the local childish folklore. It was reputed to be a poor area, and a small number of children in our class displayed evidence that there was a measure of deprivation, for these were the candidates for secondhand clothing and, I am sad to say, the target for abuse. When I, much later, ventured over the canal I found a community much like my own and one that I could, and did, easily befriend.

The first day at the new school started with assembly in which the new arrivals were welcomed, accompanied by a few ribald remarks expressed sotto voce from within the general assembly. Introduction to our class master was followed by the distribution of textbooks and a short tour of the few amenities at our disposal.

We were left with a mixture of excitement and awe and could not wait to get home to lunch to deliver our commentary on the morning's proceedings. The learning process was about to begin in earnest, and some of it was to leave me bewildered.

Not everybody in the class attended morning assembly, at which we had prayers and a hymn, followed in the classroom by a half hour of "Religious Instruction". I noticed that certain boys left before this period and did not return until it was over, the reason being that they were either Jewish or Roman Catholic. Since my only contact with such things was at Sunday-School, which I frequently avoided because I perceived inconsistencies in what they tried to teach me, I was totally confused by this practice. What I was witness to was an example of religious discrimination which coloured my approach to orthodox religion and fostered views on education generally later in life.

The first few terms established my strengths and quickly revealed my weaknesses. I had minor problems with English Grammar but was disappointed with my efforts at English Literature. My introduction to Shakespeare was limited to play-acting in class, and a larger appreciation of his work never materialised, to the extent that I failed to develop an awareness of the depth of his writing. Each term we were given a book to read and these included the works of Charles Dickens, which we were expected to read in our own time. I found this to be difficult and never was able to answer the questions that inevitably followed. I feel I was to be the loser in later life for the lack of quality in this subject, although I do not limit this criticism to myself alone because there was never any attempt to encourage a deeper understanding of either author.

French, like English, seemed to come naturally, but was restricted to the grammatical approach. I should have preferred the spoken variety that would have been of greater use when we later embarked upon a school trip to France. On the boat going across I asked for what I thought was a biscuit and drew a hoot of laughter from the assembly — whatever it was I actually said, I never found out.

I never came to terms with Mathematics. Algebra remained a mystery and I was never able to calculate how long it took the proverbial bath to fill with water. I accepted the theorem of Pythagoras but those of Euclid defied my understanding. If he said they worked and proved it, then I could see no reason why I should do so as well. The Latin "Pons Assinorum" ("Asses' Bridge") applied to one of his revelations may well have been directed at me. Notwithstanding, I did not suffer unduly in later life and was able to manage my financial and other affairs without any difficulty.

I remember one of the books that we were given was a red bound "National Song Book", that was much in evidence during the period, that went under the title of "Music", for which purpose the class assembled in the school hall, it being the only place that boasted a piano. The book contained words and music of a wide variety of songs, both folk and patriotic, and could have graced any singer's library. I must have given voice many times to "Early One Morning", bemoaned the fate of poor

"Tom Bowling" and joined the rest of the school in the annual celebration of what was then called "Empire Day", a memorable event when the whole school assembled in patriotic mood to sing, in unison if not in harmony, songs that portrayed the glory of England. The Headmaster gave us a talk, we waved our Union Jacks and were given the afternoon free of lessons. We were not, on this occasion, reminded that the country had achieved an Empire by the occasional use of force.

Such was our musical education and I now feel that the opportunity was missed to enlarge our awareness of the subject. The sound of Beethoven, or any of the classical composers, never echoed around the school hall and no effort was made to introduce us to music in general. Fortunately, my sister Dorrie, a regular visitor to the Royal Albert Hall, introduced me, through her collection of gramophone records, to the classical scene. In later life my wife established a further interest and we both enjoyed many an orchestral and choral concert in which we sometimes both took part.

In the subject of "Art" I did not display any visible talent; if any lay dormant no attempt was made to extract it and I gained nothing from many hours I must have spent in the struggle. As with my experience of the music sessions, the wider connotations of the word were not considered and the works of the great painters were never discussed, nor ever displayed around the wall. Had this formed part of the curriculum I might have shown more tolerance of what now goes under the name of "modern art", and perhaps had just a little appreciation of Picasso and Salvador Dali. In neither

Music nor Art was there any attempt to develop aesthetic appreciation of the subjects, and had they been more than just occupational exercises this might have been nurtured in, at least, some of us.

At some stage I transferred my interest from metalwork to woodwork and joined the weekly sessions — I wish it had been more. I enjoyed working with wood and was taught at an early stage to respect my tools; any slight misdemeanour in this respect brought a quick and sometimes painful response from the teacher. The proper use of tools and their maintenance was to stand me in good stead later in life. I did, however, suffer one disappointment. On one occasion I and another boy jointly headed the class and qualified for the woodwork prize, two wooden jack planes. I had hoped that we could have shared the prize as one each would have been a fair reward. It was decided that the issue should be resolved by the toss of a coin ... I LOST and was deprived of gracing the prize winners' platform.

History was a subject I never mastered. I found it dry and uninspiring and I lacked any enthusiasm for the subject. The learning of a succession of dates and events was beyond me and I never was able to meet this requirement. Apart from the Battle of Hastings in 1066, I cannot, even now, put an event to a date in history, and I am still very ignorant of any particular period from the Romans to the Tudors and Stuarts with the Dark Ages in between. I do not appear to have suffered as a result of this disability. Perhaps my inadequacy was due to nothing less than laziness that the committed historian would view with dismay. I will say, in my defence, that with the advent of radio and television I have managed to right a few wrongs.

I was aware at this time that history was being enacted around me, and the news being circulated in the 1930s was principally of the rise of one Adolph Hitler and the Third Reich in Germany, events that subsequently culminated in a Second World War, events that never became the subject of any of our history lessons.

Geography, on the other hand, I viewed as having some relevance to everyday world affairs. I enjoyed drawing maps and charts, which I did using a mapping pen and an assortment of coloured inks; I felt Geography to envisage a worldwide environment and I felt part of that structure in which the interaction of the elements with land and sea played a vital part. I am constantly reminded of the things I learnt in the Geography lessons when I view the current worldwide scene that portrays the loss of large parts of the tropical rain forests, coupled with an increasing trend of severe and unexpected weather patterns in many parts of the world. There is no doubt in my mind that my fanatic environmental concern for this planet is the fruit of the seed sown in this part of my education.

To me history never changes, but geography is continually doing so. The modern schoolboy must now, at the beginning of the twenty-first century, come to terms with global warming, worldwide famine and genetically modified crops. I wish him well, but I believe he will need to adopt a new philosophy and make sure he gets his priorities in order. Never has it been truer today that the adage "as you sow, so shall you reap" will be strictly applied to whatever he does.

One feature of this school that I had not met before was the imposition of homework. Not every subject produced this dubious pleasure, but nevertheless the time had gone when I could walk through the school gates at the end of the day and forget all about the task of learning. The amount of extra work to be done in this way was evidenced by the weight and bulging appearance of one's satchel, which is why, perhaps, the poet recognised the lad walking unwillingly to school. It was my practice to do my homework in my bedroom where I would have least interruption. By this time my sisters had married, enabling my brother and me to occupy the front bedroom downstairs. As this bordered the street I frequently, during the summer months, had to complete my task aware that my friends were enjoying their leisure in games outside. I was not likely to be allowed to join them until I assured my parents that I had "done my homework". In winter I had to transfer my activities to the kitchen. The bedroom was not heated and we were only equipped with a supply of gas, so any thought of an electric fire was soon dispelled. Central heating was a pleasure yet to come.

My school encouraged the playing of sport. In the morning, before school, we could be seen playing football in the playground; a game which normally started with a few of us, and escalated as more boys arrived into a free-for-all. If the ball did not occasionally top the school wall and land on a passing bus, it would sail over the wall separating us from the girls' school and land in their lavatories. Someone would have to stand in the doorway between us and sheepishly seek its retrieval.

The school managed to maintain a creditable team in both cricket and football, and even had lads selected for the Middlesex Boys' team. Sports results were an important feature of assembly every Monday morning and drew applause when appropriate. In class we did have sessions of football and cricket in season, but both entailed a long walk to find a suitable piece of green space, reducing our playing time considerably. Our football was played on the Wormwood Scrubs, a large open area, and it was a long walk from the school to Scrubbs Lane, from where the football pitches necessitated a further trek until we finally found a place to play. This was always with a view of the prison, a rather imposing and grim-looking edifice.

There were no amenities for our games — a pile of coats substituted for goal posts and we played without much degree of skill until our time was up. Dishevelled and with our football boots slung round our necks, we trundled back home to what reception I cannot now remember. This was schoolboys' football at the lower level, but nevertheless it was a contributory factor in producing the professional teams of the day. For many footballers this was a meagre living and a far cry from the multi-million pound figures that present-day players attract for upwards of ninety minutes' work a week . . . I can remember when Fulham and Queen's

Park Rangers players became among the first to earn ten pounds a week from their sport.

It was the practice in our school, as in many others, to have regular sessions of Physical Education, otherwise known simply as "P.E." In the Winter we would use the assembly hall, which was the only room of sufficient size to cope with a class of pupils engaged in physical jerks and running around in regulated mayhem. The hall contained the only piece of apparatus, in the form of a vaulting horse, which would dominate the centre of the room while we all queued up with the intention of taking a run in turn and leaping over it in athletic fashion. I never managed to get more than halfway and would only succeed in landing with an unceremonious plop. Fortunately for my ego I was not the only one thus endowed, and I envied those who could perform this feat.

I much preferred the summer months when we could venture outside into a spacious playground. There we would play games that developed a team spirit, and hopefully we might adopt a sense of personal responsibility and learn how to "play the game".

As young boys, my friends and I were particularly interested in the football matches played in the Wembley Stadium, not so much from the footballing aspect but because it sometimes produced an extra source of income. The Harrow Road provided a direct link from the London mainline stations to the football stadium at Wembley. Opened in 1923, some 100,000 spectators crowded into the arena to watch the first Cup Final to be played there. This particular game became known for the presence of the policeman upon a white horse who controlled the seething crowd in what might have been a recipe for disaster. Future crowd attendances were thereafter limited, and this event never again welcomed such a large crowd.

On the morning of the final each year Harrow Road became the route for scores of coaches making their way to the stadium, but our interest lay in their return journey. We would listen to the radio broadcast of the match that involved not only the commentator, but a further voice giving details of which part of the playing field was being featured in the commentary. The *Radio Times* and some newspapers printed a plan of the playing area divided into numbered squares, and the voice would say "square one" or "square four" depending on the area in which play was taking place.

When the game ended we would line the edge of the Harrow Road waiting for the arrival of the coaches on their way home. Once started, there would be an endless stream for some time, and we stood on the roadside calling out 'throw out yer mouldies' in a request for halfpennies or pennies from the occupants of the coaches. When a coin was thrown there would be a scramble to retrieve it. Of course we had some success from the supporters of the winning team who were more generous — the vanquished travelled in silence. Not only was this a feature of the Cup Final, but the stadium was also used for international football matches and this exercise became a regular feature. In all the years that I indulged in this risky venture I do not know of any mishap befalling any of us. In fact I believe that the supporters celebrating victory by hanging out of the windows and standing up in the coaches with a bottle of beer might have been in greater danger.

This was a meagre addition to an income that was otherwise provided by means of a paper round. Most of us had one; mine involved delivering newspapers and magazines seven days a week and collecting the money on Sunday morning — for which I received the princely sum of two shillings and sixpence, enough to finance my other activities.

Back at school I was about to enter a new phase in the educational process. I was approaching my third year, before which I had to make a decision that could well influence my future prospects. In addition, and by way of some light relief, I was about to join the ranks of the teenager with my thirteenth birthday, which I anticipated would give me a greater degree of personal freedom. I felt that the desire to explore and my financial security, small though it was, would enable me to roam farther afield and to see a little more of the neighbourhood in which I lived. However, I still had one hurdle to overcome.

Before entering my third year at school I was given the choice of a "Commercial" education or a "Technical" one. The former would introduce me to the new subjects of Shorthand, Typewriting and Bookkeeping, and acceptance would ensure my staying at my present establishment. The alternative would require a transfer to the Paddington Technical Institute, a school closer to my home but of which I knew absolutely nothing. There was not, as far as I was aware, any career structure advice available, and nothing resembling this was offered. I was on my own. As far as I could reason a commercial career entailed work in an office environment, commonly called a "pen-pushing job", which nevertheless provided a degree of job security if not an exciting occupation. This I knew would appeal to my parents who had memories of the depression of the 1930s, and I felt that they would be well pleased if I ventured along this path.

The alternative I knew little about — I tended to relate the technical description to the subject of Engineering, and this conjured up in my mind the vision of plans to be drawn and complicated calculations to be made. With my memories of a marked lack of prowess in the matter of the Art class, and a less than scintillating performance in the Mathematics examination, I felt very apprehensive about taking a somewhat blind leap in this direction. I therefore selected the commercial option and looked forward to the additional subjects on offer, perhaps influenced by the omission of Art lessons in the future curriculum. With the benefit of many years' hindsight and subsequent events that were to influence my future life, I have no reason to regret my decision.

I did not become very proficient in Shorthand and seemed to exhibit the same lack of manual dexterity that had plagued me in the Art class, when my reproduction of people in a bus did not depict them as persons of substance but more resembling the ghostly emanations from a country churchyard after midnight.

Typewriting was an after-school requirement, my first introduction to overtime, albeit unpaid. Covers were used to hide the keys from prying eyes and we typed exercises to music. I was better at this, and since I had the benefit of a portable typewriter at home — a present from my eldest sister upon her return from India — I became quite proficient and enjoyed the experience. Book-keeping also contained an introduction to the world of commerce, and what I learned in this direction I found of considerable value in future years when I was called upon to manage my own and family affairs. I came to appreciate the meaning of the warning of Charles Dickens' character, Mr Wilkins Micawber, of the dangers of over-spending, although his unwelcome overdraft only amounted to sixpence.

I acquired a valuable insight into the world of the moneylender, the calculation of interest and the use of Bills of Exchange. I am reminded of my mother's words, "if you cannot afford it, then do not buy it!" — perhaps a little harsh in the present day practice of "buy now — pay later". Nevertheless what I learned should be compulsory to all school students before they leave the educational arena — the overriding principles are still valid today.

Whether it was the progression into my teenage years or the development of hormonal activity I do not know, but I felt the need to spread my wings a little further than the immediate environment that had satisfied me for so long. I therefore took advantage of the excellent travel facilities that surrounded me, and the close proximity of tram, bus and the tube train enabled me to explore the great city in which I lived. Hyde Park, together with Kensington Gardens, was within easy and inexpensive reach and provided the wide-open space that I felt in need of, having been confined within an urban concrete environment for the first part of my life. The occasional visit to family relations who lived in the country were rare opportunities to see what green fields were, and I think I must have been a lover of the countryside in the embryo stage, something that would develop in later years.

Consequently it followed that I would spend some of my spare time at weekends taking a number 36 bus to Marble Arch, and after crossing the road I had the whole park to explore. From Rotten Row across the green sward to the Serpentine Lake and further into Kensington Gardens, I continued my exploration until I alighted upon one of London's oldest attractions when I arrived at that part known as "Speakers' Corner" where one could stop and listen to an oratory on a wide variety of subjects. Various speakers would set up their portable platforms and deliver forth an invitation to support their cause. I must have passed many a pleasant afternoon or evening being assailed by the representative of every political party and being invited to "join the cause". I listened to the sermons of various religious denominations, and with some I was forewarned of "impending doom" unless I changed the world, and by others I was informed that the "demon drink" could be my undoing. These were all delivered with the sincerity of their veracity, and indeed, many of the speakers went on to become revered and respected public figures in their particular discipline.

I found the experience entertaining, occasionally amusing, but above all it gave me food for thought and I was able, even at my tender age, to think about what was being said and make a comparative judgment. There were hecklers and those putting contrary points of view, but there was no violence that I saw, only good-natured discussion. Here then, was a cornerstone of our country — the freedom of speech and all it entailed, the defence of which would command our attention in the very near future.

I may have been at an impressionable age because I seemed to relate to some of the views that were being expressed and found myself turning these over in my mind in an effort to find a reason why I should not accept them. There was never any discussion at home, and neither politics nor religion became a subject for comment at the dinner table. I knew that Dad, a railwayman and trade unionist, had a leaning toward the emerging Labour movement, but no attempt was ever made to influence me in this direction. Election times were when the grown-ups assembled in small groups on street corners and heckled the supporters of one party or another, whilst we children went about singing "vote, vote, vote" for someone or another, not knowing why we were doing it. Such subjects were never raised at school, inside or outside the curriculum, and the introduction of mock elections during school hours was many years in the future.

I was becoming more conscious that I was growing up. Children's games no longer held the attraction that they once did and I was emerging as a young gentleman. I had abandoned short trousers, and I remember that my first suit included a waistcoat for which I received the birthday present of a watch and chain that I proudly displayed to all and sundry. My sisters had all married and left home and I had become an uncle for the first time at the age of eleven. Two more nephews followed at which time I stopped counting.

I began to read the newspapers, that Dad frequently brought home, which reported that some individual in Germany had risen to power. Apparently he was becoming a serious threat to my country and there was talk of war. I had, from time to time, tried to get my father to talk about his wartime experiences, but both he and my mother were reluctant to enter into any discussion on the subject. My eldest sister had helped my mother to bring up the other children and it was from her that I learned of the conditions under which my parents, and particularly my father, existed. I know that he was involved in at least one of the major battles in France and suffered a gas attack, but the subject was never raised by any of the family. My father's campaign and service medals were evidence that he had served for the whole period of the Great War, but beyond that the only information of life at home and "at the front" was that retold to me by my sister when I was much older.

From an early age I remember that my father attended many Armistice Day remembrance ceremonies in his capacity as a St John's Ambulance man and an ex-serviceman, and a framed picture of him in army uniform hung on the kitchen wall for as long as I can remember.

To a young teenager, news of possible war conjured up many images in my mind. My only introduction to the subject was provided by the penny comics and children's magazines that were read and exchanged regularly between classmates. The weekly purchase of the Rover, Wizard or Hotspur related tales of "daring-do"; of the lowly private saving his comrades with a single-handed attack on the enemy, or of the phantom footballer scoring the vital goal to win the match. At school one of my classmates had shown me a book he had acquired showing vivid pictures of scenes in France during the last war, but we viewed them more in awe than in realization of the horror involved. How could I relate to any impending war, having no knowledge of the past one and only my imagination in respect of any that there might be in the future? Yet I was a likely candidate for compulsory enlistment should the occasion arise, and the general mood was far from optimistic at this time.

There was much evidence of intense preparation should war become a reality. The creation of a Civil Defence structure produced expressions such as "Air Raid Precautions", "First Aid Post" and "Air Raid Shelter" — signs and posters being prominently displayed. Instructions followed on how to use a stirrup pump, make and fit "blackout" curtains, and where and when to collect our gas masks. Volunteers were required to man the many different posts created in this completely new experience. We were, undoubtedly, becoming well prepared on what would be known as the "Home Front" . . . could we be equally satisfied that our military preparation was equal to it? In true British spirit we were putting our faith in the Royal Navy and the Army to defend our shores. We had little knowledge of the fighting capability of the Air Force, as it had not received the same public attention as the other two services.

The news from Europe continued to worsen and the drums of war became louder. There was a general mobilization of all reservists, and I said au revoir to my brother who, as a Royal Naval Sickberth Reservist, was required to report for duty. A state of high expectancy existed, only to be relieved by further negotiations when our Prime Minister, Neville Chamberlain, departed to Germany for a personal attendance upon Adolf Hitler. He returned to Croydon Airport and, stepping from the plane, waved a piece of paper that, he said, was a signed agreement which ensured 'peace in our time'. War had been averted, tension removed and the return of mobilized troops was a welcome relief to many families, especially my own. Could we, should we, return to normal?

The projected School Journey to the continent had been cancelled because of the unstable situation in Europe. The practice of the school going abroad had been introduced two years earlier and was as much an educational excursion as a holiday. On that occasion the destination was Swansea in South Wales, where we stayed in a hotel and visited local places of interest.

Such was the success of this new venture that it was repeated in the following year with a visit to France; we stayed in Rouen for a few days before moving on to Paris for the remainder of the week. I recall little of Rouen except that I believe it had an historic connection with Joan of Arc — but then, history was never my strong point. Paris was more memorable. We stayed in a school vacated because of their annual holidays, slept in dormitories and used toilet facilities that I can only describe as primitive — but at least they were indoors and not in the school playground. We made visits to all the popular attractions, rode on the Metro, which I found comparable in all respects to our own "Underground", and took our lives in our hands when we crossed the road, having to reverse our own safety formula of looking right before stepping off the kerb. The top of the Eiffel Tower afforded memorable views and we all bought the traditional miniature souvenir. For most of us this was our first venture outside England, and for many it was not to be the last.

On return to school we were inevitably required to commit our impressions to paper, and I even managed an article on the experience for the School Magazine. My effort was well received, but I have to confess now that I was guilty of plagiarism, having seen an article in a magazine that fitted my requirements almost exactly and which I therefore scripted to my needs.

It was a relieved family that began preparation for the festivities at Christmas. It had been Mum's practice for many years to subscribe to a Christmas club run by one of the local grocers' stores, and by depositing a modest amount each week she was able to accumulate sufficient funds to pay for the extra delights that make the festive season so attractive. As the great day approached she would descend upon the store with a list prepared well in advance and return home to await delivery. While I unpacked the goods, she would carefully check that nothing had been missed, and when she was satisfied they would be set on one side until they were to be used.

It would not be long before the kitchen became a hive of activity. With the fire well stocked and the large wooden table scrubbed clean, Mum would begin an assault which produced a goodly supply of mince pies, jam tarts and cakes spread out upon the table, and if I was lucky I might be privileged to sample one. When cooled they would disappear in an assortment of tins, spirited away to await the great day.

Further preparation involved the upstairs front room that was to become the focal point of our family celebration. Normally used only on special occasions, it was necessary to remove the sheets that had covered the furniture and generally prepare the room for the family gathering. The fire would be laid ready to be lit on Christmas morning, and a supply of coal made ready in the coalscuttle, a task that, as I became older, was allotted to me. A further routine was to extract the music kept in the piano stool and place it on the piano, for its use was essential to our enjoyment. Doris and her family had decided not to return to India because of the insecurity of the international situation, and she was therefore available to accompany us on the piano. The music consisted of Victorian ballads and a volume of "Songs That Won The War".

Dad would give his usual rendering of "If Those Lips Could Only Speak", my brother's contribution being "Drink To Me Only", and my sister, who had a fine contralto voice, would give a rendering of "The Holy City". With Doris firmly implanted on the piano stool, we were set for a good evening of self-made entertainment broken only for liquid refreshment of one kind or another. We would not be the only ones celebrating in this way, and there would be ample evidence from the open windows up and down the street that our neighbours were likewise enjoying themselves. We may not have known what would befall us in the year ahead, but we would see this year out in our usual style.

New Year celebrations were, by comparison, a muted affair, but it afforded an opportunity for neighbours to get together for a sing-song around the piano before toasting in the New Year with the remnants of the Christmas spirit. Some were even to be seen joining hands in a ritual dance in the street, for these were the days when we all made our own entertainment, and frequently in a collective style.

The year 1939 heralded the approach of my last term at school and I had not any idea of what I wanted to do or be. There was no career structure in place and little advice to be had from educational sources, and so, in concert with my fellows, I registered at the Labour Exchange as being available for work. Meanwhile school lessons had developed a more informal nature, with no compulsion to learn, and relations with our teachers became more relaxed. We often engaged with them in serious discussion groups. At this time the European situation was once again giving cause for concern, and we frequently aired our juvenile views.

We were not aware of any particular qualifications that would be advantageous, and so any study we might undertake was not directed to this end. In fact, it was not until I went for interview for prospective employment that I was asked if I had "matriculated" . . . my blank stare instantly suggested that I had not. I had never heard the word before and resolved to find out more, but by then it was too late.

Employment eventually came when a former pupil of the school attended the class and gave details of a post of typist available in his firm. I considered I had a reasonable ability, and eventually I found my first job at the princely sum of one pound a week. In order to lessen the demand upon this meagre remuneration, I acquired my brother's reserve bicycle and started cycling to work. Thus ended my long association with academia.

Elsewhere the clouds of war were gathering, general mobilization was imminent and my brother was recalled to the Navy — I was to see very little of him for the next six years. In the event of hostilities, elaborate plans had been made for the evacuation of schoolchildren from the big cities, and these had come to fruition.

Throughout London children were assembling at their local schools, gas mask in a cardboard box slung from the shoulder, a label endorsed with their name pinned to their coat, and carrying a parcel or bag containing food for the journey and possibly a change of clothing. Parents looked apprehensive as they imparted last-minute instructions, before seeing their offspring transported by bus and coach to one of the main line stations.

At Paddington there were scenes that remain firm in my memory. Every departure platform was crowded with young ones, brothers and sisters holding hands tightly lest they be separated — some tearful, some even showing excitement, and all carefully and lovingly marshalled by a host of helpers. Alongside was a train waiting to transport its precious cargo to places unknown. Many had not been on a train before, nor had they seen the countryside, or the animals in it, except within the pages of a picture book.

Trains departed at regular intervals and little faces pressed against the window. The platform would then be empty until the arrival of another train when the process would be repeated. It must have been a traumatic experience for all who took part, but the smoothness of the conduct of such a mammoth operation gave credit to the careful planning that had been undertaken many months before in readiness for such an occasion. We now had to wait and see what future events would reveal . . . we did not have to wait long!

In Europe, Poland had been invaded; Germany had entered uninvited, with force of arms on the ground and in the air, in what had been described as "blitzkrieg". An ultimatum was given to Germany by the British Ambassador in Berlin laying down certain terms for peace. The result was to become evident on Sunday, 3rd September 1939 at eleven o'clock in the morning. As the appointed hour approached, my parents and I settled down to await the promised announcement. We had long since disposed of the old wireless set in favour of one of the new radios, complete with a shiny bakelite cabinet and three knobs that could be twiddled to tune in to stations in our own and other countries. We could also adjust the volume to suit our ears. It became an essential part of the furniture and was to provide sterling service in the years ahead. It was, however, powered by a battery because we had not succumbed to the attraction of "mains electricity", and Mum still preferred a dustpan and brush to the emerging electric sweeper . . . in fact, in my time living in "71" I never had the pleasure of light at the touch of a switch.

As Big Ben struck the hour of eleven, the announcer introduced the Prime Minister, Neville Chamberlain, who in solemn tone reported that Germany had not responded to our communiqué and that as a result "this country is at war with Germany". I turned the radio off and tried to assess the reaction of my parents — none was immediately forthcoming and I hesitated to break this silence, knowing that both had memories best left unstirred. Preparations for the Sunday meal were continued, until a short time later when the air raid sirens sounded.

The nation had been well prepared throughout the year for such an event and many had air raid shelters in the back garden. These were supplied to all who wanted one and consisted of a corrugated iron construction, installed half submerged in a suitable place with the excavated soil placed on top. Others, like ourselves, ventured under the stairs, which we had been assured was a reasonable alternative. No sooner had we settled than the "All Clear" sounded and we emerged to enjoy the rest of the day in comparative peace.

The following weeks seemed somewhat of an anti-climax. A British Expeditionary Force had left for France, who also had declared war on Germany, but a period of stalemate gave rise to expressions such as "phoney war" and many averred that it would all be over by Christmas. We were left to enjoy Christmas in the traditional way. Mum's routine for the festive season had not been interrupted and thoughts of war were not apparent.

It had been a dramatic year for me — I had left school, started employment and war had been declared. If the war was prolonged, it might well involve me, for I should shortly be required to register as available, if fit, for conscription, and had already made my mind up to follow in my brother's footsteps and join the Navy. Only time would tell; a decade was passing and 1940 might well be the springboard to history.

I had been a child of the thirties, an age of innocence but one of honesty, when my only crime might be riding my bicycle on the pavement and when a debt at the local store was something shameful to admit in public. Nevertheless it was an age of poverty for many, when an empty purse meant empty stomachs and the only resort was a hand-out from the Parish funds and the indignity of asking for it. We celebrated our magnificent Empire but omitted to ask why, if this country is was affluent, did some have bread and dripping for dinner? Money was in short supply, although Woolworth stores promised with the slogan "nothing over sixpence"; the fifty-shilling tailor really did produce a suit for such a price, and Mum often acquired a joint of beef for less than half-a-crown. Such things were not cheap if one only had three pounds a week and a family to keep, but the working man could still buy a pint of beer and a packet of cigarettes and get change for sixpence.

Yet for all the tribulations, these were magical times for the young. We were safe from real harm and free to roam the streets unmolested. We may have suffered painful punishment at home and at school, but beneath it all we were loved and given the best available in all the circumstances.

The Home Front

Mum had always been keen to see me in a secure job with a pension at the end of it — something which was to be expected after her efforts to ensure I had a reasonable education and, no doubt, with her own recollection of the depression years of the 1930s. With this in mind she had approached my sister Hilda's husband, Bill, who held an established position in the Post Office Engineering Department; he was able to help her to the extent that I made an application to join the Post Office in the hope of following in his footsteps. Two of my sisters had been Telephone Operators before they were married, and thus the family had already established a link with the telephone service, so my application seemed a natural development of this.

I had left school with a modest school-leaving certificate and I hoped that the lack of academic qualifications would not affect my chances of employment. After an interview in London I was accepted as a "Youth-in-Training", and, having said my farewells to my friends at the garage, I reported as directed to the Paddington Telephone Exchange on the eighth day of January 1940. I did not know then that this auspicious occasion heralded the beginning of 45 years of public service.

I was assigned to the section that dealt with the telephone apparatus on the premises of subscribers, and I was put in the charge of an established engineer who would be responsible for my day-to-day training — I went with him to subscribers' premises to attend to faults that had been reported during the day.

In addition I became a "cord boy", a job that was to become essentially my own. Within the exchange area, which stretched from Marble Arch to Maida Vale, and from Regents Park to Bayswater, there were a number of large switchboards. These were manned by telephone operators who, by means of a pair of cords, connected incoming calls to one of the many extension telephones within the building. Each cord consisted of three insulated wires within a braided cover and was connected to a brass plug; these frequently became worn and I would be called upon to effect repair or renewal. Rough handling of a cord could result in the operator receiving a mild 50-volt shock by way of a salutary warning, and so my urgent attention would be required.

As a young, fresh-faced lad I suffered some good-natured banter from the telephonists, but I soon acclimatised and had no need to hide my red face behind the switchboard. I soon became accepted and made many friends. I also acquired a good knowledge of the geography of the area and became acquainted with the local "flora and fauna" of the indigenous population. At this time a telephone was common in industry and commerce and a perquisite of the more opulent members of society; consequently I visited the more luxurious residences in the area. I particularly remember one such in Regents. Park that had its own indoor swimming pool, which to me represented the height of luxury. The headquarters of the Football Association was in Lancaster Gate, Bayswater, which I frequently visited, but I never plucked up courage to ask for a Cup Final ticket.

In addition to the training I was receiving from my mentor, I was required to attend the Post Office training school where I was taught the manual dexterity involved in handling delicate equipment, and the basics of wiring, jointing and general maintenance. I was further encouraged to attend evening classes at the local technical college which provided courses to City and Guilds standards in Magnetism and Electricity, and in Telephony. As an incentive, success in these disciplines would earn me an extra four shillings a week for the first two certificates I obtained at Grade One level, a welcome bonus to my basic weekly wage of fifteen shillings. Notwithstanding my prior unwillingness to follow a technical education, I found I had an aptitude for the subject and that I enjoyed learning.

It had been a hard winter and the snow appeared to have limited hostilities in France. As far as I was concerned, the snow helped me to find my way around in the blackout. The absence of street lighting created an eerie atmosphere in which sound was magnified, and tiny points of light could herald the approach of vehicle, bicycle or a fellow pedestrian following a narrow beam from their torch. Neighbours went unrecognized, and one occasionally collided with a fellow traveller, both expressing profuse apologies.

From time to time an unfortunate resident allowed their blackout curtains to emit a small beam of light, which drew a stern injunction from the patrolling Air Raid Warden to "put that light out!!" One did not argue with an ARP warden.

As a nation we were much dependent on imports of food and materials, and shipping would be threatened and supplies endangered if the war went on for any length of time. A form of rationing was imposed, which varied at first and later settled down to a familiar pattern. The weekly ration we were allowed consisted of:

8 ounces of Fat (including 2 ounces of Butter)
2 ounces of Tea
8 ounces of Sugar
1 ounce of Cheese
4 ounces of Bacon

Meat, initially rationed by price alone, was later included at one shilling and ten-pence worth a week . . . and that included the bone. Sausages were a rarity and when available soon produced a long queue of excited housewives. Those engaged in heavy industry received larger allowances, and there were also special arrangements for the very young. To obtain what one was entitled to involved registering with a supplier of one's choice, something that produced a little healthy competition in the marketplace along the Harrow Road.

Television was still something of a novelty and very few people possessed a set. It was only in black and white, and, being very expensive, was beyond the means of the majority ... the service was duly suspended at the outbreak of the war. The wireless was the principal medium for the news, while the cinema remained a popular source of light entertainment where one could, for sixpence or ninepence, escape reality for a couple of hours or more, even though this might entail queueing outside. It would be a generous programme of an "A" and "B" film, a cartoon and the news (Pathe Gazette), supported in the interval by a live band that alternated between two local cinemas and provided musical entertainment. Theatres in London did suspend activities for a time, but resumed and were well attended. The Windmill Theatre maintained its slogan "We never close," and, in fact, never did so throughout the period of hostilities.

It was to the wireless that we turned for our creature comforts, and it became the linchpin to maintaining our morale as we adjusted to a strange new way of life. The wireless was to become a vital link for entertainment, news and information. For example, it enabled harassed housewives to cope with the limitations imposed by rationing by producing simple and nutritious recipes sprinkled with a little encouragement along the way. One such was for "Woolton Pie", a wholly vegetable concoction named after the then Minister for Food. Other recipes followed using dried egg powder — a favourite of mine as it produced what I considered a reasonable breakfast meal, a view not always shared by others. Improvisation was the order of the day and, with occasional encouragement from the experts, we survived, slimmer perhaps but fit enough to see us through.

Much reliability was placed upon the wireless for up-to-date news, although certain items were intentionally delayed for reasons of security. This was particularly so when news of losses at sea were withheld so that the next-of-kin could be informed. The sinking of the Navy's ships used to send a shiver up my spine as the report was usually prefaced with the words "the Admiralty announces with regret", and with bated breath I waited to discover which ship had suffered. I felt a certain rapport with this Service, having a brother currently serving and hoping to follow him myself.

The wireless also provided some lighter moments in its concern for our welfare and we were regularly treated to the advice of the "Radio Doctor", Dr Charles Hill. It was he who encouraged us to eat plenty of prunes, which he called his "black coated friends" and which would have an efficacious effect upon the bowels. His frequent broadcasts showed much concern for our physical health and his amusing anecdotes added a little humour. It also became the practice of announcers to give their names before reading the news; the voices of Alvar Liddell and Bruce Belfrage became instantly recognizable and they became our unseen friends.

It was in the field of light entertainment that the wireless became a dominant factor with a distinct emphasis on humour, an important element in the maintaining of morale. A portent of what was to come was portrayed by a programme called Garrison Theatre, featuring Jack Warner. He was destined to become popular with his imaginary "Letter from my blue pencil brother Sid", so-called because the letters were reputed to contain many obliterations in blue pencil of anything written that might be of help to the enemy — this being the recognized method of censorship of mail from the armed forces. The expression came to be adopted generally as a convenient substitute for an expletive. Such comedy programmes spawned many catchphrases which became an important ingredient in maintaining our morale in the months ahead.

On the "Home Front" things were comparatively quiet but there were signs that the phoney war was coming to an end. There had already been attacks on shipping in coastal waters with, sadly, loss of lives and ships. The Royal Navy had lost a battleship, the Royal Oak torpedoed by a German submarine in Scapa Flow. Scapa Flow had been seen as an impregnable base for the Navy's Ships in two wars, and infiltration was believed to be impossible. As a result, entry was immediately limited by blocking all but the main entrances to this vast natural harbour. A further loss of a capital ship occurred when HMS Courageous, an aircraft carrier, was sunk in the Western Approaches some 170 miles off Ireland. The considerable loss of life that was sustained on both occasions was an understandable blow to morale.

In France there had been very little activity. French forces were, to all belief, safely encamped behind the fortress known as the Maginot Line, an elaborate system of fortifications linked together, pointing eastwards towards Germany and extending the entire length of the Franco-German border. The British Expeditionary Force was arrayed along the Franco-Belgian border and we waited for the phoney war to end. It did so in dramatic form . . . Germany invaded both Denmark and Norway. Britain sent an expeditionary force to aid the Norwegians, but they were ill equipped to face the German forces and a tactical evacuation was ordered.

The war was on the point of escalating when, on 10th May 1940, Germany, without warning, invaded Holland and Belgium with vastly superior forces. Neville Chamberlain, already under pressure following the debacle in Norway, was left in no doubt when a member of his own party, quoting Oliver Cromwell, said, "You have sat here too long for any good you have been doing; depart, I say, and let us have done with you. IN THE NAME OF GOD, GO!" Later that day he tendered his resignation. The King invited Winston Churchill to become Prime Minister. He accepted, and a National Government of all parties was formed.

The German Army advanced through Belgium and into France, thereby circumventing the much-vaunted Maginot Line and rendering it totally ineffective. The French Army became trapped behind it and was unable to relieve the pressure upon the British Forces along the Belgian border. What followed has been well chronicled, dissected and analysed by subsequent historians; sufficient to say that it terminated upon the beaches of Dunkirk. The subsequent appeal for ships brought an unexpected and sudden response. Pleasure boats, week-end cruisers and a fleet of privately-owned craft were brilliantly organized into an armada of ships and, supported by the Royal Navy, succeeded in retrieving some 350,000 British and French troops in day/night operations that astounded the world.

There were memorable scenes at harbours along the south coast as ships of all shapes and sizes disembarked their cargo of dishevelled and tired troops, unshaven and clutching the remnants of their belongings, while willing hands offered the relief of a cigarette and a mug of tea — the first for many days. The whole operation was viewed as one that ranked with the rout of the Spanish Armada for its sheer audacity in the face of the enemy and which prompted Winston Churchill to address the nation on the wireless when he said ". . . The battle of France is over, the battle of Britain begins. So let us brace ourselves to the task and so bear ourselves that men will say, this was their finest hour".

Soon afterwards, Italy declared war on the side of Germany, and France sought terms for peace, setting up a form of Government in Vichy in the South of France. We now stood alone in the fight for freedom — German forces were arrayed against us along the entire length of the French coastline, and the intervention of

Italy would have serious repercussions in the Mediterranean.

Talk focused upon the likelihood of invasion, and a call went out for the formation of what might be called a civilian army. The Local Defence Volunteer force (L.D.V.) was officially created and open to all men above the age of 17 who, for one reason or another, were not eligible for military service. For its first few months it boasted no uniform, save an "L.D.V." armband, while its weaponry consisted of what one's best imagination could create.

I joined as soon as I became eligible. The GPO had its own unit and we were attached to the City of London Battalion of the Royal Fusiliers. Uniforms and weapons subsequently arrived, and we were re-named the "Home Guard". Our instructors were, invariably, veterans of the 1914–1918 war, and we were taught arms drill, bayonet practice and how to disarm a tank with a hand grenade. I fired a Lee-Enfield rifle for the first time, and the "kick" of the recoil nearly took the weapon out of my hand . . . but the young generation was full of enthusiasm.

Britain continued to make preparations for a likely invasion across the Channel. Roadblocks were prepared for immediate use should the need arise, and concrete gun emplacements, known as "pill boxes", appeared in strategic places throughout Southern England. On the coast beaches were mined, and access denied by the judicious use of coils of barbed wire, our holiday bathing virtually curtailed for the duration. In fact, many of the restrictions were "for the duration", and any complaint drew the retort, "Don't you know there's a war on". Railway Station name boards were removed, signposts taken away or obliterated, and no efforts were spared to confuse the enemy. In spite of all the preparations, I did not share the view that invasion was imminent. I felt that the presence of the Royal Navy and the Royal Air Force would be sufficient deterrent to immediate action. The German High Command must have had similar views because they launched an assault upon our defences in an effort to gain command of the air — a necessary prerequisite to any venture across the Channel.

August saw the beginning of bombing raids on Coastal Radar Stations and airfields in the South of England, and the Royal Air Force and the Luftwaffe became engaged in almost continual combat. High in the sky, RAF pilots, often outnumbered, fought pitched battles in what was to become known as the Battle of Britain. Throughout southern England spectators stood and watched as the tell-tale vapour trails and rat-tat-tat of machine-gun fire told of the drama being enacted thousands of feet above. The full impact of the effect this drama would have upon this country's fortune would not be appreciated until later when our pilots, many peacetime leisure flyers, others young reservists, would earn the accolade of Winston Churchill when he said, "Never in the field of human conflict was so much owed by so many to so few". It gave a boost to the country's morale and thoughts of invasion receded into the background.

We had, almost daily, been given a running total of our successes in the air during the Battle of Britain, and the news that 185 enemy planes had been destroyed in a single day seemed to represent the climax of the battle, although this figure was amended downwards at some later date. Raids did continue, but reduced in intensity, and for a short time our attention was focused on other areas of conflict.

The fall of France had effectively exposed the whole of the North Sea coast to German occupation. As this country was so dependent on imports of food and raw materials, command of the high seas and protection of shipping was of vital importance to our survival. Germany had, since coming into being as the Third Reich, steadily built up its naval potential with emphasis on the submarine (the Unterseeboot or "U-Boat") and the pocket battleships developed as swift, armed raiders. These had been deployed in the Atlantic Ocean before hostilities and, once war had been declared, became an instant threat to shipping. The pocket battleship Graf Spee had already destroyed a large amount of merchant shipping before its eventual self-destruction after a battle with the Royal Navy off the coast of South America.

To combat the threat of the U-Boat a system of shipping in convoy under naval protection was introduced and a new phase of the war was beginning. The "Battle of Britain" was to be followed by the "Battle of the Atlantic". In the meantime there was more to come on the home front too!

The Blitz

I think it is fair to say that the abiding memory of Londoners and of those living in other large cities is their experience of the "Blitz". The term is a shortened version of the German word Blitzkrieg, or "lightning war", a description given to the speed and power of conquest much in evidence as Germany made territorial demands upon her neighbours Holland and Belgium.

The Spanish Civil War had in 1937 already given witness to the targeting of civilian populations by air strikes, and the First World War had produced limited attacks from the Zeppelin airship. The possibility of the use of poison gas by this means had prompted the issue of gas masks to the entire population, designed for adults, children and young babies. It became compulsory to carry them at all times and the little brown cardboard box became a feature of everyday apparel — I did not find it comfortable to wear. As a further measure we were encouraged to drape a dampened blanket over doorways as additional protection, but this was a measure that not many people followed, no doubt considering it to be a step too far alongside the current weight of restrictions we were gallantly bearing.

The threat of invasion seemed to have receded with the failure of the enemy to overpower our Air Force, and the existence of our Navy would further deter any attempt to land on our shores. Nevertheless, there was sporadic bombing in southern England and bombs were dropped without any pattern emerging — this being reported in the news bulletins as "bombs dropped at random". Meanwhile, James Joyce, a former English public schoolboy and now resident in Germany, regularly broadcast messages and statements from a radio station in Hamburg, which were designed to undermine our well-being. With a markedly affected accent, which earned him the nick-name of "Lord Haw-Haw", he would report the effects of bombing raids by naming the target towns and to which he frequently added "Random was also bombed" as if "Random" was a town in Great Britain. He was not taken seriously and became a butt for comedians and impersonators. At the end of the war he was charged with treason and paid the penalty.

The German high command, apparently having abandoned plans for immediate invasion of these shores, was poised to make a more direct attack on this country. For those living in London the next few months would bring the front line closer to home. The 7th of September 1940, as I remember, offered a pleasant sunny afternoon when, at about teatime, the shrill ululating sound of the air-raid sirens broke the tranquility of the day, Londoners prepared to take cover and the trek to the air-raid shelters began. We had no prepared arrangements and Mum and Dad seemed content to remain in the house. Some of our neighbours had erected Anderson shelters in their small back gardens, and there were brick-built surface shelters available, but these were uncomfortable and had no sanitary facilities. A sense of fatalism developed (if a bomb has your name on it . . .) and many seemed willing to "take a chance".

The sirens had sounded but nothing appeared to be happening in our part of London. However, gradually news filtered through that the London Docks had "got it" — meaning they were the obvious target of the raid. After a short break the sirens sounded again and the attack continued. The extent was not to become apparent until nightfall when, as the skies gradually darkened, a red glow appeared in the sky, which became more intense and remained visible throughout the night, to be replaced as dawn broke by a pall of black smoke hanging over the dockland area. The attack on the London Docks was to be a prelude to over 70 consecutive nights when the capital was bombed and which would provide an abiding memory of the war to all Londoners who witnessed it.

Areas of high population density, such as the East End of London, were next to be targeted, which resulted in a much higher incidence of casualties. Horrendous scenes following a night's raid became commonplace, and everywhere there could be seen the aftermath of the night's visit with piles of rubble, and Civil Defence workers striving to reach the victims.

Amongst the carnage there were some oddly humorous sights, such as a building sliced in half and the pictures still hanging on the wall, or a bath still attached to the plumbing but otherwise suspended in space. If there was anything to raise a smile the hardy East Ender could be guaranteed to find it, and it was not unusual to find a shattered shop front bearing a notice which read "a bit more open than usual" and the motto, "business as usual".

Following the bombing on the East End of London, the German bombers diverted their attention to the remaining suburbs of the capital. As darkness fell one anticipated the rise and fall of the air-raid siren and, as the daylight hours became shorter, so the raids began earlier. After the initial warning, a period of quiet would follow until gradually the heavy drone of aircraft engines signalled their approach and the noise of anti-aircraft fire broke the expectant silence. It became a matter of waiting to see if they would continue overhead or whether the whistle of their bombs signified you might be their target. It was said that if one heard its approach it could be close, but if you did not, it would be too close for comfort. An exploding bomb nearby would cause a ripple of vibration to be felt underfoot and, although a strange sensation, it was one we became used to.

A variety of bombs were dropped during these raids. Generally they consisted of incendiaries to illuminate a target, followed by high explosives (HE) delivered in sticks of perhaps four or more bombs in quick succession for maximum damage or destruction.

Incendiary devices burnt fiercely on impact and were capable of starting a fire in a matter of seconds. They were frequently dropped in large clusters. There was also a very high explosive device, comparable to a marine mine, delivered by parachute and whose silent approach and considerable damage potential caused them to be feared. Occasionally they became entangled in trees or on telephone wires, which would cause a mass evacuation of the immediate neighbourhood until they exploded. One could pass them by in the black-out without being aware of their close proximity, and they were often not discovered until morning light.

Although we were subject to nightly visitation I was able to spend some time in bed and occasionally was left undisturbed. There were, however, other noises that were guaranteed to interrupt my sleep. Opposite No.71 was a small road linking Portnall Road with an adjoining road, which contained only two houses, with frontages onto the street. Virtually free of traffic, it had been an ideal playground for me when younger, and provided both makeshift football and cricket pitches upon which we played according to the season, subject of course to the intervention of the local friendly constabulary. As there was little available open space in the neighbourhood for the establishment of fixed anti-aircraft units, it became the practice to have mobile support in the form of a Naval gun mounted upon a suitably adapted vehicle. This would patrol the area during an air raid, and the road opposite was well suited for its purpose, but the noise created when it discharged its wares was enough to "awaken the dead" and snatched me from the "arms of Morpheus" in no uncertain manner on more than one occasion.

It was business as usual for most people, although an overnight visitation from the enemy could mean disruption on journeys to and from work. Roads that were used daily would be denied to us, or we would have to walk amongst the rubble of bombed buildings while Civil Defence workers strove to clear the carnage of the night before. Travel by train for those commuting into London could mean a delayed journey, while the evening return could mean sitting patiently in a darkened carriage while outside the sky would be lit up by a display of bursting anti-aircraft shells and wavering searchlights accompanied by the sound of the guns.

As telephone engineers, my colleagues and I were kept busy renewing lines to vital services, which sometime tested our ingenuity to find the best route to lay fresh cables through damaged buildings to link with those engineers having a similar problem in the street. Morale generally remained high and the inconveniences suffered as part of daily life and the oft repeated phrase that "there's a war on" was accepted as some form of consolation. The shared dangers saw the removal of barriers of race, colour and creed, and a sense of community developed which affected young and old, rich and poor alike.

In spite of the dangers, cinemas and dance halls were well attended, and the arrival of an air raid would be communicated to those taking part but there was seldom any attempt at mass evacuation, most being content to remain until things became too close for comfort. Sporting activities were, however, disrupted as many who took part had enlisted in the armed services, and in addition nighttime events such as speedway and dog-racing were closed down for the duration because of the ban on the use of floodlights.

But there were signs that the assault was, at least for the time being, coming to an end as the enemy diverted their attention to other parts of the country.

The relaxing of the nightly assault enabled a little more concentration on what was available on the wireless for our entertainment. The service from the British Broadcasting Corporation (BBC) had, following upon the outbreak of the war, been reduced to a single channel called the "Home Service", which was transmitted on Long and Medium frequencies from 7.00 a.m. until midnight when the service closed down. A service for those in the armed forces was broadcast on a separate channel.

The programmes available on the Home Service varied and included a selection of plays, concerts of both orchestral and light music and, for younger listeners, Children's Hour, although this was reduced in length. The Forces frequency also included comedy programmes, one of which, High Gang, featured Bebe Daniels and Ben Lyon, a husband and wife team from America, broadcasting programmes that linked service-men and women with their families at home. There was some criticism of the BBC, which questioned the broadcast of comedy at such a serious time for the country, while other critics questioned the overuse of patriotic songs on the wireless. Morale during the period both before and after the bombing of the capital was possibly at its lowest ebb throughout the years of the war, and the need for some comedy was welcomed and became a regular feature with programmes directed to different branches of the armed forces.

New programmes rapidly developed, and in one in particular, "Private" Jack Warner became the first new variety star in a very successful "canteen" show called Garrison Theatre, which demonstrated the appeal of simple comedy. It may also have established the use of the catch-phrase with the weekly entrance of Jack Warner, wheeling a bicycle and shouting, "Mind my Bike". The catch-phrase style of humour caught on and became a feature of many programmes to come. One show in particular was It's That Man Again, commonly known as ITMA, featuring Tommy Handley and a host of supporting talent. The charlady, who supposedly cleaned the office, would enter with a raucous enquiry of "Can I do you now, Sir?" while the diver declared in a solemn fatalistic tone, "I'm going down now, Sir". It was quick-fire repartee and the public loved it.

Letters sent home by members of the armed forces were sometimes subject to censorship and the censor would utilize a blue pencil to obliterate any material that might breach national security. It was not long before the expression "blue pencil" was adopted as a catch-phrase, to replace a choice expletive and to give emphasis without the use of strong language.

A Ministry of Information was set up to regulate much of the news released to the public and it was required to strike a balance between the need to know and the maintenance of morale. The loss of ships at sea was not publicly announced until the next of kin had been informed, and sometimes, for strategic purposes, the news was not released until much later or even after the duration of hostilities. The Ministry was also responsible for the devising and issuing of posters on a variety of subjects of national concern, which were prominently displayed throughout the country. One such poster was directed to those who might have access to sensitive information and emphasized the need for secrecy with such slogans as "Careless Talk Costs Lives" and "Be Like Dad, Keep Mum". Others encouraged the joining of the armed services with a "King and Country" style plea much in evidence, apparently, during the First World War. But the wireless was to develop a vital service for those in the occupied countries.

Following upon the occupation of much of Europe by the German Army, groups of men and woman formed themselves into groups with the avowed intent to disrupt the occupying forces at every opportunity. Such groups became known collectively as "the Resistance" and were to be found in all the territories under German occupation. If the resistance was to achieve a maximum effectiveness it was necessary that they were provided with a point in the free world upon which they could focus and co-ordinate their efforts. Such a means was set up in this country and the BBC was to play a prime role.

The operations of the resistance groups were, of necessity, clandestine; the risks they took were considerable and the penalties upon being discovered were severe in the extreme. Some groups were able to communicate by short-wave wireless, which they carefully concealed from discovery, and in this way sought the supply of arms and expertise. This often resulted in the delivery of arms by parachute and also, occasionally, the delivery of a human cargo. Messages to the underground resistance movement were effected through the BBC wavelengths and delivered in code, sometimes amusing, with a meaning known to only one particular group. It became the practice to introduce this service by a signal of three dots and a dash (. . . -) representing the morse code for the letter "V", signifying "Victory", which soon became a symbol throughout the occupied countries as a signal of unity in defeat. It was perhaps ironic that this was also the opening rhythm of Beethoven's Fifth Symphony and the work of a German composer.

A welcome hiatus in bombing activity enabled us to lick our wounds, but it was not destined to last long. At the end of November German bombers turned their attention to other targets with heavy raids on Coventry, Liverpool, Southampton and other cities. Coventry, in particular, was subjected to an eleven-hour assault resulting in heavy damage and loss of life. The cathedral was decimated, and although a modern edifice later arose from the ruins, a solitary bomb-scarred wall was left standing as a memorial to those that died. A new word, "Coventrated", was coined and frequently used to mean any heavy bombing attack.

The approach of Christmas did not invoke the usual feeling of expectancy. The complete lack of festive lighting in the streets and shops, casualties of the black-out, and the absence of members of the family in the Forces gave little reason to feel in a celebratory mood. We had, the previous Christmas, raided the store cupboard and almost exhausted our supplies of good things, and the onset of strict rationing had not enabled it to be replenished. There was no possibility of the usual rich Christmas fare, although the Ministry of Food did its best and introduced a variety of substitute recipes. One such, for Christmas Pudding, required the use of carrots, breadcrumbs and a small measure of dried fruit, with the garnish of creams utilizing a little margarine and dried milk. I suspect a liberal helping of imagination was the final ingredient. Mum had always made her own puddings and mincemeat at this time of the year, but I think on this occasion we preferred to go without.

The year ended with a devastating attack on the City of London when that part of the capital, commonly referred to as the "square mile", was severely damaged in a deluge of incendiary bombs. This part of the City, with its narrow streets and historic buildings, was engulfed in fire and smoke above which the cathedral of St Paul's remained largely intact although many of Wren's famous churches and the Guildhall succumbed to the flames. Fire services from all parts of London strove to contain the conflagration against overwhelming odds, and the scenes the following day were of heart-rending proportion. It is no surprise that the occasion earned the description of the "Second Great Fire of London", in which the survival of St Paul's was attributed to its voluntary "fire watch" scheme involving both staff and friends who were able to deal with the incendiary bombs and so prevent the spread of fire in the building.

As the raid was carried out on a Sunday night most of the business offices were unattended and the fires were able to spread unhindered. This prompted the swift formation of the National Fire Service and the Fire Guard; those civilians not already involved in the Home Guard or ARP were ordered to undertake fire-watching duties, generally at their place of work. As a member of the Home Guard I was not required to join, but I did so and took part in the protection of my local telephone exchange in Paddington with regular night-time vigils.

The break in the bombing pattern had been short lived and further attacks followed. They tended to be delivered in phases, the present one principally at night, and the targets varied, with towns over the whole of the United Kingdom being visited by the Luftwaffe, many on repeated occasions, resulting in much damage and loss of life. On one raid the German bombers targeted the London mainline railways and every station sustained some damage. Paddington was no exception when a bomb tore through the glass roof of Isambard Brunel's edifice and exploded between platforms five and six. Damage was limited and services were soon restored.

Living in close proximity to the railway line it was not surprising that bombs would fall close by, and one landed in the road not far from us. It severely damaged the house of a former classmate of mine and in the morning his mother, intent on providing for the family, returned and started to prepare breakfast, only to be interrupted by a Civil Defence worker who enquired what she thought she was doing as the house was in a dangerous condition and had been condemned. I never knew whether the family did get their breakfast but I know that, sometime later, one of the family made a clandestine return in order to retrieve their supply of coal in the cellar.

Raids continued on random targets with varying degrees of intensity, with a final assault at the end of May when seaports and the industrial heartland received the attention of German bombers. It had been my practice, during an air raid, to venture out in Home Guard uniform, complete with a tin helmet, to patrol the neighbourhood in the hope that I might be of some use to the Civil Defence workers. On one such occasion I came upon a small group of men attempting to extract a casualty from the basement of the BBC studios in Delaware Road that had received a direct hit. It was a cold night and I covered the casualty with my army greatcoat as we carried him into the building. I retrieved my property the next day. The studios, initially built as a skating palace, were taken over by the BBC for concert broadcasting and are still in use today. Through their records I have been able to ascertain the date of this incident as 11th May 1941 at 2.14 am. On another occasion I joined a group of workers and watched helplessly as a local church burned while the fire services were heavily committed by incendiary attacks elsewhere in London.

That raid was the final fling against London — it was estimated that 500 planes dropped tons of high explosive and incendiaries, causing many people to be killed or injured. More than 2,000 separate fires were started and their glow again lit up the London skyline. The capital's railway termini were also hit, together with bridges across the Thames; many homes and factories were also casualties, making an estimated 12,000 people homeless. There were some who expressed the view that these attacks were intended to soften up the population as a prelude to the invasion. It never materialized because Germany, notwithstanding a non-aggression pact with Russia, turned its sights eastwards and promptly invaded that country.

The relief from continuous bombing enabled me to focus my attention on the other theatres of war. The daily news reported fighting in Greece and in North Africa, where British and Commonwealth Forces were engaged against Italian forces who had invaded both territories soon after their entry into the war, but it seemed too far away to warrant my concern. There was a more worrying situation developing closer to home that would threaten our existence and the means to wage war. Since the occupation of France the Germans had built concrete submarine pens from which they mounted repeated assaults against merchant shipping bringing much needed food and materials across the

Atlantic Ocean. Although formed into convoys and protected by the Royal Navy, the German submarines, often operating in packs, were successful in destroying thousands of tons of shipping with the loss of many lives. The speed of any convoy was limited to that of the slowest member, which added to the task of the escort ships, while putting the faster ships at greater risk of torpedo attack.

Repercussions were naturally reflected in life on the Home Front and were to have an effect upon our food supply. The meat ration was reduced, and by June had settled at one shilling (5p) worth each week for each person holding a ration book. It was reported at the time that Winston Churchill, when shown the amount of meat, considered it to be an adequate amount for a meal for one person, that is, until he was told it was the weekly ration and not the daily allowance as he had thought. Jam and marmalade were added to the list, followed by cheese, which was limited to two ounces a week. Vegetarians were allowed extra but forfeited their ration of meat. A National Loaf was introduced and, although wholesome, was grey in colour and a little gritty to the palate. Tea became in short supply and the practice of allowing "one for the pot" was discouraged.

In order to supplement our allowances we were encouraged by a "Dig for Victory" campaign to turn our gardens into vegetable plots, and another poster appeared to take its place alongside the many that already existed in public areas. Cherished lawns and flowerbeds across the country were turned into miniature market gardens to produce a supply of potatoes, carrots and a variety of other vegetables to supplement the food ration. Much hallowed turf in sports arenas throughout the country came under threat of being sacrificed, for the duration, to the common cause. I suspect there may have been much study of seed catalogues and gardening literature as a new generation of avid gardeners became established. Even our small suburban garden made a modest contribution although I cannot now remember what we grew.

New Horizons

The previous months may have occupied much of my attention but they did not curtail my activities. I had, by now, taken full ownership of my brother's old cycle and my mother, ever mindful of my safety, had relented and allowed me to use it to cycle to work. I soon also acquired my brother's enthusiasm for the sport and I ventured farther afield with weekend visits to my two sisters, Elsie and Hilda, who lived in adjoining roads in Hayes, Kent, part of a large estate that was one of several housing developments springing up in the outer environs of London. I also went westwards to a delightful spot in the country at Burnham Beeches in Buckinghamshire, taking the opportunity of calling upon my aunt and uncle who lived close by.

Uncle Arthur, after whom I may have been named, was Dad's brother and lived with Auntie Emily in a small cottage with primitive sanitation and no electricity but with a delightful garden. Uncle Art, as I knew him, had worked on the land for most of his life and cultivated the garden, and I would return home with a saddlebag bursting with the fruits of his labours. The supply of petrol, being restricted to those directly engaged in the war effort, had reduced the volume of traffic on the roads and I invariably shared the return journey with the occasional Army lorry. I sometimes indulged in a friendly competitive ride with other members of the cycling fraternity on the way home. In common with my brother, I joined the Cyclist's Touring Club, an organization founded in 1887 to champion the cycling tradition, and of which we both subsequently became Life Members.

Activities in the Home Guard continued even though the need for this additional defence force may have lessened when the fear of invasion departed. We frequently carried out exercises among the rubble of bombsites, which followed upon the devastation of the city, and what we lacked in expertise we made up for in enthusiasm. With other members of our Platoon, I regularly did a guard duty in the Paddington Telephone Exchange when our Lieutenant in Command would occasionally pay a surprise visit to keep us alert during a seemingly long and tedious night. I remember on one occasion, a colleague, upon the entry of the Officer, attempted to "present arms" in the traditional manner, raising the rifle smartly before lowering it in salute. Unfortunately the bayonet attached to the rifle became firmly embedded in the ceiling, leaving the rifle suspended in space. No longer holding the rifle, he had the presence of mind to bring his hand smartly to his forehead and achieve a salute in a more usual way. Thereafter fixed bayonets were not required when mounting guard inside a building!

I was now approaching the age when I should be required to register for conscription into one of the armed services, or, as ten percent of lads were, into the coal mining industry. I hoped that I would not become a "Bevin Boy" — named after one Ernest Bevin, a Member of Parliament — and spend the rest of the war down a coalmine. At the outbreak of war the age for compulsory service was 20, but this was reduced to 18 following the losses in France before "Dunkirk". My eighteenth birthday loomed large upon the horizon and I registered when my time came to do so, but before I could be enlisted I was required to attend for a medical examination. This followed soon after, although I cannot now remember where.

I assembled with about 20 other potential recruits, and the event is still fresh in my mind. We found ourselves in a large hall with several cubicles erected along one wall, each containing a member of the medical profession complete with an item of medical paraphernalia. We were invited to remove all our clothes, which we did, and proceeded, a naked crocodile of flowering youth, to visit each cubicle in turn to be prodded and poked, turned and twisted, until we emerged at the other end. Having retrieved our clothes we were called to a top table to learn whether we were fit enough to fight or be destined to return to our usual occupation.

To my pleasure I was declared A1 and my potential as a future sailor was established if not yet determined. All I had to do now was wait for the little brown envelope that reputedly would contain an invitation that I could not refuse. In the meantime I had to exercise patience, which I found difficult, especially when I saw my contemporaries proudly parading their newly acquired uniforms when they came home on their first leave. Of course they did not tell me what those first few months were really like . . . I was to find that out myself in due time.

Until then I had other things to occupy my mind and divert my energies elsewhere. My time as a trainee telephone engineer on the subscriber side of the service came to an end when I was transferred into the exchange at Paddington to learn the intricacies of the automatic telephone system.

I did not take kindly to being denied the freedom I had found in the outdoor life, and I took some time to settle down among the noisy and confined atmosphere of the very large rooms containing a variety of equipment and the mechanical clatter it created. In addition, because of the nature of the equipment, windows were not to be opened and reliance was placed upon a ventilation system that I found produced more dust than fresh air. However I had arrived thus to complete my learning process and not to criticize my environment and, with the benefit of a good training structure within the Engineering Department, I subsequently enjoyed doing so.

My object was to obtain qualifications in Telephony from the City and Guilds of London Institute, and to this end I purchased a volume on the subject written by Messrs Herbert & Proctor that was recommended reading for all budding engineers. "Herbert and

Proctor", as it became known, was generally accepted as the engineers' "Bible", and most of my colleagues possessed a copy.

The building in St Michael's Street, Paddington, was in fact the home of two telephone exchanges — Paddington and Ambassador. Both were fully automatic exchanges using the "Strowger" automatic switching system (or the "girl-less, cuss-less telephone") which, we are told in a British Telecommunications Museum Publication — "Museum Briefing No.1" — was the work of an American, Almon Brown Strowger (1839–1902), an undertaker by trade who, motivated by the lack of privacy in operator-connected telephone calls, invented an automatic switching system that did away with the operator.

Strowger did not invent a fully automatic exchange, but the two most important basic elements of such a thing — the rotary selector (an electrically operated switch which, under instructions from a caller, connected them to one of a number of a curved bank of contacts) and a calling device by means of which a caller could send strings of pulses to control the operation of the selectors. The original system took many improvements before it was sufficiently practical for general use.

The dial, as we now know it, was added in 1896, followed eight years later by a further switching process, the linefinder, or as I would know it the uni-selector. When a caller lifted their handset, their linefinder detected that they wished to make a call, and connected them to a number of Group Selectors through which they could dial their call. In this way the more devices there were in an exchange determined the number of calls it could deal with at any one time, and not by the number of subscribers connected to it.

The introduction of the Dial Tone gave an indication to the caller when the equipment was ready to make a call — in practice the wait was fractions of a second. By 1924 Britain had 26,500 lines working on 23 automatic exchanges — Paddington and Ambassador were known to each have an ultimate capacity for 10,000 lines. The Strowger system proved flexible and versatile and reached a peak in 1980, and it was made in Britain. Shortly afterwards digital systems started to come into use and the end of Strowger became a matter of time as exchanges were converted.

I was being trained to maintain the electro-mechanical switches and also to understand the complex circuitry that made the whole thing possible. With the aid of first class training facilities provided by the Post Office Engineering Department, and the impetus of a City & Guild's Certificate, I enjoyed doing so. The era of the Manual Telephone Exchange utilizing large switchboards and many operators for local calls was coming to an end, but the services of an operator were still required for calls beyond the local area and overseas. The centralized "Toll" and "Trunk" exchanges remained but the era of universal Subscriber Trunk Dialling (SDT) was something on the distant horizon.

Once established inside the exchange I made new friends, one of whom was Jack Burgess, a young lad of my own age who, like me, cycled to work and also for pleasure. We were both in the position of waiting to be called up; Jack setting his ambition on becoming a pilot in the Royal Air Force while I had hopes of entering the Royal Navy. We became cycling companions, getting on our bikes at every opportunity, especially at weekends. Jack lived in Hammersmith, a short ride away. I would cycle to his home and together we would venture into the highways and byways of the distant countryside.

A supply of food and drink in our saddlebags, and using a quarter-inch Bartholomew's map — sign-posts, if not already removed, may have been altered to confuse an enemy and so were unreliable — we found our way through the leafy lanes of Surrey or Buckinghamshire. On the way home we would call at a roadside café for a cup of tea and a homemade cake, where we would often meet fellow two-wheel knights of the road and discuss our day's adventures.

There was an unmistakable fraternity among club cyclists everywhere one went on two wheels, and with little traffic to hinder us, cycling was a most pleasurable pastime — and it kept us fit at no extra cost. Occasionally we would take a tent and enjoy a camping weekend in a quiet riverside spot — a primitive exercise for we cooked our food on the traditional wood fire, taking care to observe the Country Code and leave every site as we would wish to find it.

My brother had become a married man earlier in the year to Ivy Bilham, who became known to us as "Billie". He was a Sick Berth Attendant in a Royal Naval Hospital outside Edinburgh, and I had seen very little of him since the beginning of the war. I remember little of the marriage ceremony in January, except that there was snow on the ground around the little church in Wembley, but I do remember that he had been courting a young lady who had also fulfilled the role of rear seat "stoker" on his tandem that now lay unused in the downstairs passage at home.

I had kept the tandem in good order and now decided I could put it to good use. I cannot remember whether I asked his permission, or if it was granted, but I occasionally rode it single-handed to pick up Jack for a daily spin. Two young and fit lads together on a bicycle built for two presented a formidable combination and with the open road beckoning we would cover quite some distance, easily achieving 100 miles in one day. It was not unknown for us to overtake the occasional slower vehicle, but in all the time we cycled together we never had, or caused, any misfortune.

Apart from our cycling expeditions we also shared Home Guard and Fire Watching duties, to which we brought the same youthful enthusiasm, and we generally enjoyed ourselves while waiting for that little brown envelope that would augur our call-up into the Forces. We had, however, been told that the work we did was classified as "war work" and could delay our ultimate call-up — news that did not please me at all.

Meanwhile, on the Home Front the relief from endless air raids, together with the German invasion of Russia, appeared to show that the threat of invasion had passed and was no longer a matter of concern. I felt that the war had reached a state of impasse. The country had been on the receiving end for the past two years and we had reached the stage where it was necessary to recoup our losses. We were in no position to mount any consolidated attack, which would of necessity involve the invasion of France, because we had not the heavily armed force that would be required. Looking further afield, British and Commonwealth forces were engaged in the Middle East and in North Africa against combined Italian and German forces. The news from the Atlantic arena was more hopeful, and we were finding some success against the German U-Boat menace, which meant that vital supplies were reaching us in greater quantities.

The United States of America had adopted what was known as an "isolationist policy" with regard to the war in Europe and had no wish to become involved. However, they were prepared to supply this country with the materials of war, which supplemented the production of armaments in our own factories throughout the country. Factories that once produced a range of British-made cars now saw assembly lines turned over to the production of military vehicles and tanks, while the cotton and woollen industries were engaged in the manufacture of uniforms in khaki and two shades of blue.

The expression "War Work" now had real meaning and saw women being recruited to take their place in heavy industry alongside their male counterparts in factories throughout the country. Music was introduced into factory life and loudspeakers relayed the latest tunes to the workers, and during the lunch-break they would be entertained by an impromptu stage show in the works canteen. Such shows were sometimes broadcast on the wireless under the title of Workers' Playtime.

With the loss of much of the workforce to the armed services, the role of women became of paramount importance. Instead of being viewed as the weaker sex they were now being seen in roles of some variety, from driving heavy vehicles to working long hours on farms in the Women's Land Army — no longer the petite, demure image of femininity but an essential cog in the overall war effort machine.

Personally I felt I was in limbo — an intermediate state of waiting for something positive to happen. The overall news of the war was not encouraging. The Russians were in retreat in the face of the German onslaught, and in North Africa the small success we had achieved had been reversed by the appearance of one Field Marshal Rommel to lead the German troops. Nearer to home the Navy had succeeded in sinking the German Battleship Bismarck but at the cost of our own HMS Hood that had exploded with the tragic loss of most of its crew. I felt that we were in for a very long war.

Mum and Dad were a stabilising influence on me as they carried on without emotion or complaint. They had both been in a similar situation and still had memories of the Great War; I think they understood my sense of frustration and never condemned me for my occasional outbursts. It was not until much later that I realised the pain they must have suffered at my desire to leave home and join the armed forces. They already had one son in the Royal Navy and seeing their other one straining at the leash must have caused a little hurt. Having served in France during 1914 to 1918, Dad understood my feelings and counselled patience — he had always been a steadying influence, calm and unhurried, and if ever he had to return home for something he had forgotten to take with him, he would make a point of sitting down and counting to ten before he ventured out again. I have suffered pangs of conscience ever since.

I was, however, able to direct some of my pent-up energy into my work in the exchange, which I was finding extremely interesting. Although I had opted for a commercial type of education when I was at school I had now plunged into the world of Telephone Engineering and I found it fascinating. I was learning the secrets of how the dialling of three letters and a number could enable one person to call another anywhere in London — calls further afield were not yet available by dialling and still required the services of a telephone operator.

Telephone numbers were preceded by the name of the local Exchange, reduced to the first three letters. Hence subscribers in the Paddington area would be identified by the name of the Exchange and the number allotted to their individual line. Subscribers elsewhere who had the dialling facility would dial PAD followed by the number of the person they wished to call. Names of Telephone Exchanges frequently followed the name of their locality or its geography. Those adjoining my own particular area were MAYfair,

REGent and GROsvenor, all situated in a single building in a most salubrious area of the West End of London — there were Exchanges named North and East, but no South or West. Eventually I came to know all the London exchanges and where they were.

The telephone operators who were necessary for long distance calls occupied the whole of the top floor, where a large switchboard with many operators was situated and from which they could connect subscribers to many parts of this country and also overseas. Operators were specially selected for clarity of speech and underwent strict training before taking their place on a large switchboard. They had a dialogue of their own and, with two sisters who had been operators, I had become acquainted with the phraseology that they were required to use and especially the ability to roll their "Rs" in speaking, which seemed to be a feature of the profession.

But it was not all work and no play. No longer under the threat of disruption by air raids, it became a pleasure to visit the "pictures", and Mum, Dad and I would occasionally take our places in the queue for the ninepenny seats, or if it was shorter, the sixpenny queue, although this one attracted the younger generation who liked to be close to the front, especially in the "cowboy and Indian" films, where they no doubt felt part of the action. If we wanted a special treat we could pay a little more and go upstairs, across the lush carpeting, into the "upper circle" — a venue for which it was not generally necessary to queue.

An evening at the cinema was always good value for money, with two films, a "Mickey Mouse" or other cartoon and an interval when we would be entertained by a live band or an organist playing the traditional cinema organ that rose from the depths as he played the latest tunes. A special attraction was always the "Pathe Gazette" or "Movietone News" that provided a filmed presentation of home and world events which invariably featured scenes from the various theatres of war and brought the conflict a little closer to home.

Alternatively the "wireless" was our companion for a quiet evening and there was entertainment to suit all tastes, with light and classical music, comedy and a play. The kitchen front was not ignored and recipes to help the harassed housewife were presented, although the speed with which they were read led to complaints, as a letter (to the "Radio Times, May 1941") reflected — "that their wonderful recipes are quite useless if the unfortunate listeners have only time to jot down portions of them".

On a pleasant summer's evening we occasionally took the bus to Hyde Park for a leisurely walk around the Serpentine Lake, a popular venue for Londoners and visitors alike since early Victorian times. The lake dates from early 1700 and was achieved by damming the Westbourne Stream as it flowed through the park on its way to the Thames. Another interesting feature of Hyde Park was Rotten Row — a stretch of sandy track running along one side of the park. The name is thought to have been derived from the French "Route Du Roi" and typified the use to which it was put, as it

103

was the frequent venue of the 19th century aristocracy and a place where it was appropriate to be seen in one's carriage or even on horseback.

It was also the site of the Great Exhibition of 1851, from which the glass exhibition building was afterwards removed and re-created in South London as the Crystal Palace. Unfortunately it was destroyed by fire in 1936, leaving only the two tall towers unharmed, but these were later demolished (1940), as they would have been landmarks for approaching enemy bombers.

By now I had become accustomed to the changing face of my surroundings. As more men and women enlisted into the armed forces, so there was visible evidence in the streets. The young man who lived further up the road, and who I regularly saw as I cycled to work each day, had now been transformed into the smart soldier in uniform proudly walking home on leave. There was a general increase in the number of men and women to be seen in khaki or a shade of blue, while the young ladies seemed to enjoy being seen on the arm of a soldier, sailor or airman.

Dance halls had been forced to dispense with the strict requirement of shiny dancing pumps in favour of footwear that was clearly "army issue", and many had taken steps to protect the once hallowed surface of the ballroom. I was never adept in the art of ballroom dancing but the sight of a pair of army boots attempting a delicate chasse would cause me to fear for the safety of a young girl's toes. Nevertheless the uniform continued to attract the ladies who would like to be seen with a military escort where a little gold braid would be an added attraction. My humble Home Guard attire could not compete in an unequal contest.

With the supply of petrol strictly controlled and restricted to those vehicles deemed "necessary for the war effort" the volume of road traffic diminished, which I, as a cyclist, welcomed, although there was a gradual increase in the volume of military traffic, especially in the rural areas where Army and Air Force camps were being set up to accommodate the growing numbers of service personnel. The growth was nowhere more evident than in the London mainline stations where there was an almost continuous movement of troops travelling between camps or on leave. Wherever there was a large concentration of service personnel one would see the tell-tale caps of the Military Police who always appeared to tower above everyone else. The army police became known as Red Caps because of the distinct colour of their headgear, while their Naval equivalent could be identified by their white belts and gaiters. Both seemed to have large feet and a slow, measured and unhurried step that, so I was told, was intended to strike fear in the heart of the young recruit — both, I was assured, were best avoided if possible. One day I might find out for myself!

On 7th of December 1941 came the startling news that the United States Pacific fleet, anchored in the base of Pearl Harbour, had been the target of a surprise attack by a large force of Japanese aircraft. Based upon a fleet of Aircraft Carriers, waves of bombers succeeded in causing immense damage and destruction to the might of the American Navy in the Pacific Ocean and there was no doubt that the attack had caught the strategic base completely unawares. This assault was immediately followed by a Japanese declaration of war on both the United States of America and Britain, and the invasion of Thailand and Malaysia. Germany and Italy lost no time in making a similar declaration of war upon America. The Isolationist policy, which America had defended for so long, was totally in ruins and Britain no longer stood alone — the alliance of the two countries thereafter became known as the 'Allies'.

The Japanese offensive continued without a break, and shortly after two of Britain's battleships, HMS Prince of Wales and Repulse, were sunk in the Pacific Ocean. Japanese forces also turned their attentions to the Philippines — and it was not yet Christmas. In the space of a few days the face of war had changed and I viewed the impending New Year with some apprehension.

Fortunately my mind was focused on events closer to home. Early in the New Year I had completed my two-year period of youth training in the Post Office telephones and had been rewarded with a promotion to become an "Unestablished Skilled Workman", for which my pay packet would be increased by five shillings a week. Under the rules then existing, the period of being unestablished was to last for five years, of which one half only would count towards a qualifying period for a retirement pension at the end of my service. Telephone engineers, although recognized as being in Government employment in the General Post Office, were not considered to be Civil Servants but were categorized within the "Minor and Manipulative Grade" of the Civil Service. Their classification as workmen reflected their status as "blue collar" manual workers. I have, ever since, nurtured a grievance that an engineer, trained and skilled in the intricacies of the telephone system, should be so derogated. As "workmen" we commenced work at 8.00a.m. until 5.45p.m. — white collar workers commenced their duties at 9.00a.m. and finished at 5.00p.m. . . . and they received higher wages.

It was not uncommon for a young lad to be transferred to another telephone exchange on completion of his period of youth training, and I was no exception. I found myself in the Victoria Exchange, a short walk from the mainline Southern Railway station, an exchange with a similar system of working to that at Paddington. The building was also the site of the former manual exchange called "Franklin", which still contained the old manual type of switchboard and associated equipment and which now stood, a relic of the past, bathed in the gathering dust — I found it a convenient place to leave my bicycle while I was working.

I still had much to learn, but my older colleagues were helpful and, together with excellent training facilities, I quickly learned the intricacies of the telephone system. I seemed to relate easily to the demands made upon me, and found my work both fascinating and interesting. But there were other demands upon the skill of the telephone engineer, by the armed services, and in particular by the Royal

Corps of Signals who had responsibility for the communications network in the field. The conscription of eligible men from the Post Office could not be long delayed. It was some compensation that women were being recruited to perform the more routine and less skilled work in the exchange and they became an essential part of the workforce.

The entry of America into the war should have served as a boost to morale, but I felt that the general population viewed the event with a mixture of suspicion and relief. Little was generally known about the large continent on the other side of the Atlantic Ocean. With a policy of not becoming directly involved in anything beyond their shores they posed something of an enigma to the man in the street. Most people may have become acquainted with the story of George Washington, a cherry tree and an axe, and the victory of truth over falsity, but beyond that most would profess some ignorance of that country. To the younger generation, America meant the world of the cowboy and the Indian, in which the cowboy always won — the white man was always portrayed as superior. We were about to meet the Americans in large numbers, in close proximity and some might be coloured.

Their appearance was, initially, a slow process but they came with a considerable reinforcement to our military capability. It was said, rather unkindly, that they had come over to win the war for us, but this sentiment may have been a mere echo of a similar comment made in 1917, during the Great War. Although the general feeling may have been one of goodwill, the British serviceman did not greet the physical appearance of American personnel with loud acclaim. Relationships were strained by the lavish spending of money and by rumours that the United States' troops got their bacon fried in butter and served up with two eggs. I suspect the British Tommy seldom saw either.

The Americans were, without doubt, an attraction for the ladies who were soon captivated with gifts of nylons, cigarettes and chocolate. Their smart uniforms of light khaki compared favourably with the rather drab issue of the British serviceman. Lavishly decorated with a variety of strips, badges and other insignia and with a fine line of charming conversation, they had little difficulty in attracting willing ladies to escort around town. The overall response was reflected in the comment that "they were overpaid, over-sexed and over here!"

I watched their drill routine when I occasionally visited Hyde Park, and found their style carefree and casual and, in my view, no comparison with the well-disciplined performance of the British soldier, sailor and airman, achieved after much "square bashing" at the hands of an enthusiastic drill sergeant. The Home Guard could also display a creditable performance, as I know from personal experience at the hands of a First World War infantry sergeant.

The American authorities took great steps to make their servicemen feel "at home" and we saw the arrival of the big bands of America with vocalists and instrumentalists that, previously, we had only known by reputation. American servicemen's clubs featured such artists as Benny Goodman (clarinet), Harry James (trumpet) and their bands, and Glenn Miller, whose band had a style all their own and became among the most popular performers for both American and British alike. Everything American appeared to be bigger and grander and it took a little time for this diminutive island to come to terms with this transformation but, whether we called them Yanks, Doughboys or GIs (Government Issue) they were here to stay and we were going to be glad they came.

The time was approaching when I should be thinking of taking a holiday and I was well aware that this could be the last opportunity before I was summoned to a vacation at Government expense, with full board and uniform at no extra cost. Holidays did not appear in many people's curriculum; coastal resorts in the South of England had been heavily fortified against invasion, and sandy beaches had given way to large structures to deter the landing of enemy craft, or they had been barricaded and mined. Hotels and boarding houses had, in many cases, closed for the duration and those that remained required a contribution from our ration books in order to produce a reasonable holiday fare. Some had been taken over for military occupation, frequently for the accommodation of officer rank.

On my small budget I could not subscribe to a boarding house, and hotels were a luxury I certainly could not afford. I needed a cheap holiday and was quite willing to forgo some of the usual comforts. There was but one solution — I would go camping. Jack

Burgess, my cycling companion, was in a similar situation and readily acceded to my idea — we decided a tour of the county of Devon would be acceptable. With a tandem in the downstairs passage at home that was adequately equipped for our purpose with panniers and saddlebag, it was only left for us to plan a cheap excursion to the West Country. Although we worked in different telephone exchanges we were able to arrange our leave and set a date for our departure in July.

Having loaded the bike with my requirements, I cycled to pick up Jack, who was supplying the camping gear and sleeping bags, which we loaded, together with his own needs, safely on to the tandem. We had ridden part of our route many times on our weekly excursions into the countryside and, with little traffic on the road, we two fit lads made good progress. We stopped only when we could find a suitable tearoom or café for a short rest and refreshment.

We had not intended to make the entire journey in one day and the time came when we should be looking for overnight accommodation but this was to prove more difficult than either of us had foreseen. Many likely places appeared to be closed or had no room for two hungry and tiring cyclists and it became a question of journeying from village to village until we reached the small town of Mere in Wiltshire. We must have presented a sorry spectacle as two lonely cyclists stood beside a well-laden bicycle. I thought that the local Police Station might, just possibly, allow us the comfort of one of the cells and an enquiry to a passing local resident placed us in the right direction. They were most hospitable and referred us to an address a little way down the road, to a lady, they said, who once provided bed and breakfast and accommodated overnight travellers in her little cottage.

It was now getting dark as we tentatively knocked on the door, which was opened by a white-haired lady. Confronted with two slightly dishevelled and grubby young men, it would not have been surprising if she had not hurriedly closed the door, but fortunately for us she was well acquainted with members of the cycling fraternity and welcomed us in. She wasted no time in providing us with the means to refresh ourselves while she prepared a welcome meal before showing us a comfortable bed. Her welcome hospitality continued with a hearty breakfast to send us on our way, and I think she only charged us two shillings and sixpence (12½p). Needless to say we thanked her and booked a return visit for our stop on the way home.

Continuing on our journey we slipped into the tranquillity of the West Country, with its seemingly unhurried pace and the slow Devonshire drawl far removed from the bustle of the capital. We resisted the temptation to divert from our route to view the cathedral city of Exeter. It had recently been the target of German bombers in what had become known as the "Baedeker" raids. The RAF had mounted air attacks on a number of German cities, which provoked a response in the form of low-level, retaliatory raids upon the cathedral cities of York, Norwich and Exeter amongst others, and we did not wish to view their distress. Instead we cycled on, taking a left turn somewhere along the road towards the south Devon coast and began looking for a suitable place to pitch the tent for a week.

We came upon a likely site alongside the road in a little place called Dawlish Warren which would afford us a base for further exploration of this delightful county. Discovering that the owner lived in the adjacent house, we explained that we were both expecting a call to the services and had taken this opportunity for a last minute holiday and would he let us camp in his field. Whether we had touched his sense of patriotism or generosity I do not know, but in any event, we obtained his permission to camp, free of charge. He also offered us the facility of obtaining our provisions from the farmhouse, for which we were very grateful. Beyond the field lay a wood that we knew would provide the necessary fuel for a campfire, so we lost no time in settling in and brewing a welcome cup of tea. A cold-water tap in the farmyard provided our washing facilities, but we did not mind such a Spartan existence, after all it was part of the joy of life under canvas.

We spent the rest of the week exploring the towns and villages along the Devon coast. We tackled the steep hills around Teignmouth and followed the river through country lanes to villages with the strange-sounding names of Combeinteignhead and Coffinswell, and on to the pretty little bay of Babbacombe where we negotiated the steep hairpin bend down to the beach. Here we found no impediment to a bathe in the crystal clear water.

In the evenings we relaxed in a quaint little pub at Starcross, only a few minutes walk from where we were camped. Sampling the local brew of strong cider, known as scrumpy, we sat and listened to the songs rendered by the local inhabitants. The locals were very interested in the "two young lads from Lunnon" although they may have felt us a little odd for cycling all that way when we could have come by train. Nevertheless they kept us amused with their singing and stories delivered in their lovely West Country accent. At closing time we walked (unsteadily?) back to our sleeping bags and an uninterrupted sleep.

We had left the tandem stored in the barn overnight, which perhaps was just as well. However, not all went quite to plan. Returning to our campsite after one of our daily excursions we found the tent no longer standing and our belongings laying scattered around. Not knowing the cause of the mini disaster, we could only just stare, lost for words, until we collected ourselves and began to remedy the situation. A few words at the farmhouse soon revealed the culprits to be two young pigs that the farmer had let loose in the field, and they, in the search for food, had been the purveyors of our distress. It had always been our practice never to leave much food in the tent and the pigs must have laboured in vain. We got a sympathetic apology with the observation that "Ay, that be pigs for ee" — but the farmer also added further advice not to leave our prized bicycle in the barn for fear it would be kicked to destruction by the horse. We pleaded the

114

ignorance of two city boys, offered up a silent prayer and prepared to retrace our steps and head for home.

We broke our return journey with a further visit to our lady in Mere and arrived home, tired but with a sense of achievement — and the bicycle behaved impeccably throughout. There had been no little brown envelope awaiting either of us, but we had not long to wait and the next phase of our young lives was not far away.

Back in the real world I soon got back into the regular routine, and as summer gave way to the season of mists and mellow fruitfulness so the news on the military fronts began to take a turn for the better. In North Africa a new offensive had begun at a place called El Alamein and appeared to be heading for some success, while reports from the Russian front suggested an offensive by Russian forces was having similar success. With the continuing build-up of forces in this country, I began to wonder if my services would, after all, be required. Meanwhile I was learning the virtue of patience.

But then came the news from a jubilant Jack Burgess that he had received his call-up and was heading for the Royal Air Force as he had wished. I saw him on his first leave, resplendent in his pale blue uniform with a white flash in his cap signifying his acceptance for officer training. We corresponded for a time until he went to India when I then lost track of him and I, too, was bound elsewhere.

Eventually my daily vigil behind the upstairs letterbox was rewarded by the appearance of the brown envelope addressed to me. I took it, unopened, downstairs so that I might reveal its contents in front of my parents. Simply, it said I was to report to HMS Royal Arthur at Skegness in Lincolnshire. It gave me the date, the fare and the times of the trains — I was in the Navy, as I had hoped! Nevertheless, I was having a pang of conscience. Much as I was pleased to be able to play my part in this war, I felt I was deserting my aged parents. Veterans of one war and now with two sons in the next one, I felt they were not only a little frail, but vulnerable and in need of my companionship. If they felt this, they never once revealed their feelings and gave me every encouragement. My instructions further required that I took a suitcase with me in order that my civilian clothes could be returned to my home — I sensed a strong feeling of finality in this last injunction.

I decided to carry on working until the last day as a civilian and went through my usual daily routine at the Exchange. One of these necessitated the cooperation of telephone operators at the end of the line, and during a conversation with one I mentioned my forthcoming entry into the Navy. We were completely unknown to each other but she offered to write to me while I was away, an offer I readily accepted. We arranged a meeting that evening and chose as a central location the booking hall at Trafalgar Square underground station where we made a brief acquaintance and exchanged names and addresses — it truly was a "brief encounter" and was to be a milestone in my life which, together with my later years, was to fashion the future for me. My days as a civilian were about to end, at least for the time being, and a new era about to start.

Under the White Ensign

HMS Royal Arthur

I was not entirely unaware of what lay before me when I joined the Navy. My brother, a former reservist, was already serving and had, from time to time, acquainted me with some of the vagaries of naval life so that I was not apprehensive as I stood on the platform waiting to board the train to Skegness. My father came to see me off, and my last recollection as I left the station was of him standing, a lonely-looking figure, giving me a gentle wave that epitomized his very nature. I must admit that I shed a tear as I wondered what must have been going through his mind as he watched me depart. The memory is with me still.

I remember very little of the journey save that, having to change stations, I saw the unmistakable square tower of, what I was told, was the Boston Stump, which, my informant enlightened me, was in fact a church. I was not able to contradict him. When I alighted at Skegness station my fellow recruits were easily identified by their suitcases and with a measure of bewilderment that I must have shared. We were rounded up, rather like lost sheep, by a kindly shepherd bearing the crossed anchor of a Petty Officer who led us outside to a large vehicle bearing the initials RN, and he invited us to "jump on the wagon lads". Five-ton Royal Navy lorries are not the most comfortable means of transport and so I was thankful that the journey was a short one along the coast.

Our destination appeared to be a conurbation of buildings of various proportions stretched along the road and fronted by a large open area that contained a flag-pole from which fluttered the White Ensign, (the Cross of St George with a small Union Jack in one corner), the traditional flag of the Royal Navy. Once inside, we alighted and were ushered into a nearby building. Our names were checked and a short speech of welcome was followed by an invitation to acquaint ourselves with our new surroundings and to return in time for the evening meal.

We wandered, tightly packed for fear of getting lost, and somewhat bemused at the frequent tannoyed instructions which must have meant something to someone or other. The rear of the camp consisted of innumerable small shed-like buildings that appeared, by the coming and going of the inhabitants, to be some form of habitation. I ventured to make an enquiry of a passing sailor who was apparently well versed in the origins of my new home and who enlightened me that the site was opened as a holiday camp in 1936, an innovation of a Mr Billy Butlin. This new style of holiday provided full-board accommodation and entertainment all on one site, together with its own

119

stretch of sand and sea. Soon after the declaration of war it was taken over by the Admiralty and became HMS Royal Arthur, now being used by men and women to enter the service and receive basic training before joining ships or other training establishments. My fount of all knowledge also told me that the first Royal Arthur was a vessel with full sail laid down and completed in 1893 — I was standing on board the second to receive the name. By the end of the war more than 250,000 personnel had passed through.

Having retraced its steps, our little party was ushered into a small room and served with an evening meal. I recollect it was a form of meat stew, and most acceptable it was, after which we were introduced to our sleeping quarters for the night. This comprised a dormitory-type room with double bunk beds upon which nestled most inviting six-inch thick mattresses that met with my instant approval — if this is the standard of comfort, then I am glad I joined!

I slept soundly that night until that time of a morning when the dawn was about to break the darkness of the night. I was awakened by a bugle call, which signalled the end of all our slumbers, a fact soon confirmed by the raucous tones of our mentor inviting us to "Wakey, Wakey, lash up and stow", an injunction I was to hear many times in the future. Our morning ablutions taken care of in our comfortable surroundings with plenty of hot water, we proceeded to breakfast, after which we assembled ready for our first full day as ordinary seamen.

I was given the opportunity to express a preference for any particular branch of the Navy — without of course any guarantee that it would be met. Anticipating this occasion, my brother had already given me a little advice and, on his recommendation, I stated my preference for the Radio Mechanics branch. I had to undergo a number of intelligence tests to determine my capability for completing the intense training course that I was told was necessary. I must have passed them, for I was subsequently accepted as a trainee to begin after my basic training at Royal Arthur had been completed.

Within the next few days the reception formalities were completed and I was introduced to my accommodation — a wooden structure containing an iron bunk bed, but no running water or heating and no six-inch mattress . . . and I had to share this palatial palace with one of my comrades. The uniform was the traditional "square rig" and consisted of bell-bottomed trousers, and a jumper that was so tight fitting it required assistance in order to extricate oneself. The bell-bottoms were devised during the days of sail to allow them to be rolled up to the knee when swabbing the deck with water, but I was never called upon to test their efficiency in this respect. They had a flap instead of a fly opening, and no pockets. A two-inch wide canvas money belt was also issued which contained a receptacle for small change. Additional adornments consisted of a blue collar with three white stripes on the edge, which, contrary to popular belief, did not represent the three victories of Admiral Nelson.

The ensemble was completed by the addition of a "silk", folded into three and hung around the neck, and a white lanyard. True to tradition the silk represented the rag with which early sailors used to wipe the perspiration from their faces, while the lanyard only appeared on the occasion when one was dressed in one's best suit, traditionally known as number ones. To complete my kit I acquired a hammock (complete with a palliasse and a blanket), a kit bag and a pair of boot brushes, all of which were stamped with my name and number.

After our initial issue we were required to provide for our future requirements and to repair and wash (dhobi) our own clothes. We received a small allowance in addition to our pay that could be spent in the clothing store, familiarly known as "slops", to renew any that were beyond repair. Periods of time were allowed for this process, which became known as "make do and mend", and the times were regularly "piped" through the tannoy system.

The Spartan nature of our accommodation was reflected in the facilities for our daily ablutions. Situated a short walk away, the "Heads", as they were known, comprised a long hut with a row of sinks on one side and a row of lavatories on the other. There was provision for lighting, but the electric bulbs had long disappeared and we had to provide our own and remember to remove it when we had finished our routine. The sinks were devoid of plugs and, if we wanted a decent wash, we had to provide one of these as well. By the time I arrived for my morning wash and shave the water was barely warm, the supply of hot nearly exhausted by the early risers, of which I was never one, and I managed to shave by peering into the remains of what was once a presentable mirror. A coke brazier that had been installed at the entrance to protect the pipes from freezing provided the only heating but we were forbidden to stand over it for fear of inhaling the dangerous fumes.

In just a few days I had been transformed from a civilian to become an Ordinary Telegraphist, number P/JX 674233 — the P indicating that I had become a rating of the Portsmouth Division; there were other divisions at Devonport (D) and Chatham (C). I was now fully equipped, including having been vaccinated and inoculated against most known diseases, to begin my basic training. This was to be dominated by the exercise known as "square bashing" and involved various manoeuvres of marching in all directions in slow and quick time, with and without a rifle. The overall effect, apart from implanting a measure of smartness in my turnout, served to give me an appetite for dinner and contribute to the wearing out of my boot leather.

By way of relief we were regularly engaged upon an exercise known as "work ship" which entailed being detailed to perform various jobs around the camp, varying from the movement of coal to the sweeping of the parade ground, and included the cleaning of the "Heads", all of which were designed, no doubt, to instill a sense of discipline within us. Even our dreamless sleep was not left undisturbed. We took our turn in mounting a watch, which always seemed to be in the middle of the night, and entailed climbing a vertical ladder to keep watch from the roof of one of the larger buildings. Peering into the darkness that hung above the North Sea and facing a cold east wind was a pleasure I would have willingly foregone. However, at the end of two hours a reward was to be had in the galley (kitchen) in the form of a steaming hot cup of pusser's kye, otherwise known as cocoa, and which had a thin film of grease floating on top — but it tasted good and thawed out the frozen extremities.

It has been said that King Alfred the Great, renowned for having burnt the cakes, was responsible for the creation of the British Navy, which always had a tradition all its own. It has developed its own phraseology from the early days of sail, and I think it was this mystique, still much in evidence, that attracted me to the service.

A perquisite much enjoyed by members of the lower deck in the Navy was the daily issue of rum. Commonly called "grog", the term is said to emanate from "Old Grog", the name given to Admiral Vernon (because of his habit of wearing a Grogham cloak) who, in 1740, first served diluted, instead of neat, rum to sailors. The dilution, in my time, was one part of rum to two parts of water — commonly called "two and one", to distinguish it from the allowance to Petty Officers and above who had neat rum for their daily issue. For those who chose not to partake of this little luxury, there was a very small financial benefit allowed in lieu, which supplemented an already very small weekly "wage". There was a special time at which the ration was distributed. Shortly before the midday meal one would hear the tannoy pipe "up spirits", at which time those entitled to their rum ration would assemble and duly receive, under strict supervision, this heart-warming beverage. I believe officers retired to their Wardroom for something a shade stronger.

An additional traditional privilege enjoyed by the Navy was the issue of a tobacco ration. This took the form of pipe, hand rolling, or leaf tobacco, and although not free of charge was very good value for the small amount paid. I have no doubt that this particular facility started many on the road to an addictive habit, but it was to be many years before the association with public health was recognized.

Following upon the issue of the tobacco ration there would be much evening activity on the mess-deck when it was common to see little piles of tobacco and diligent sailors rolling it into usable cigarettes, stowing the finished product in their small tins. This gave the opportunity for a smoke when it was not possible to go through the routine of rolling one, and it avoided any delay in the process. There was always a ready market for any surplus to one's own requirements and an opportunity to supplement one's pay. It also had the effect of encouraging non-smokers to take up the habit, and I was not excluded.

The mess deck was comprised within a large building, which I imagined could have accommodated some form of sporting activity, but now served as a dining hall — more commonly called the mess deck.

Furnished with long tables and chairs, it could easily accommodate 1,000 hungry sailors at mealtimes, and in the evening became the venue for a little relaxation when one could catch up on letter writing or spin a few yarns with fellow shipmates. A little background music of the latest dance tunes was added to provide a mirage of tranquility — the chalets in which we slept were cold, ill furnished and not conductive to any form of relaxation.

Alternatively one could, when permitted, take the "liberty boat" ashore, which, translated, meant a walk into neighbouring Skegness or the local village of Ingoldmells, but I preferred to indulge this privilege at the weekend, when in common with others I could descend upon the nearest fish and chip shop and follow it with a walk round the town.

I had soon discovered that the large open space where the White Ensign fluttered was known as the Quarterdeck, a somewhat hallowed area upon which one did not walk unless it was in marching order. Any other reason for traversing had to be accomplished at the double — failure to do so invariably produced an echoed reprimand from whoever in authority had witnessed the misdemeanour. This area featured largely in the Sunday morning routine when the ship's company would parade, in our best uniforms (No. 1s) in a ceremony known as "Divisions". I cannot now remember the exact sequence of events, except that a Royal Marines Band accompanied our exit from the parade ground. I was most impressed by the band and have since become an admirer and supporter of their music. After divisions we would be required to run around part of the establishment as a means of gentle exercise — another relic of the days when sailors on board ship had little opportunity or space for exercise.

With the approach of the festive season my thoughts naturally turned to the possibility of Christmas leave. I had already enjoyed one leave period since I joined and had been able to establish acquaintance with my new girlfriend, with whom I regularly exchanged letters as we had promised. On that occasion she had met me at the station and I took her home to introduce her to my parents; I sensed that they saw her as a threat to the time available to them, but they said nothing. I cannot now recall whether I did manage to get home for Christmas or whether, in accordance with tradition, I had my turkey and trimmings served to me by the ship's officers in the bleak surroundings of the mess deck. In any event, I was coming to the end of my initial training and my thoughts were directed to my next port of call when I hoped to commence my Radio Mechanic's training.

I did not have long to wait. The certificate of my service in the Royal Navy, issued to me when I was eventually demobilized, shows that I departed for HMS Shrapnel in February — and a new phase in my life had begun.

My short time at Royal Arthur had taught me something; I now knew how to march in a straight line, how to lash and stow my hammock with the traditional "seven seas" hitches, and how to salute in the Royal Naval fashion of shortest way up and shortest way down; I had also been introduced to the native dialect of the "Scouser" from Liverpool and the "Geordie" from Tyneside. I found them to be great characters, but I still have difficulty in understanding their lingo! I had earned seven days leave at the end of the "square bashing" experience and took my final leave with hammock on my shoulder, kit bag under my arm and the ticket to London clenched firmly in my teeth. Officers were denied the traditional salute.

I welcomed the opportunity to spend time with my parents and to catch up on the family news, especially of my brother, who I discovered had been drafted to HMS Woodpecker, but whose precise whereabouts could only be guessed. I made a point of calling in to see Dad at the ARP office at Paddington station, because I knew he derived great pleasure in showing off his two sons whenever he had the opportunity. I did not mind being introduced as the "baby of the family" — after all, I was still not yet twenty-one.

I was also able to renew acquaintance with Joan, my lady friend with whom I had maintained a steady correspondence. Together we ventured into the West End of London and enjoyed a visit to the Royal Albert Hall, where I was introduced to the delights of classical music, and we were also able to take advantage of the servicemen's clubs for additional entertainment. The influx of American troops had continued apace and they had brought their culture, their big bands and their own source of entertainment to the Metropolis.

HMS Shrapnel

All too soon my leave was over and I now had the task of transporting my bed, my entire wardrobe and myself to Euston station for the journey to Rugby, my next port of call. Mainline stations in wartime could adequately be described as a hive of activity in which I was one of the inconspicuous bees. Men and women in khaki and two shades of blue, many like myself carrying the burden of all they possessed, strove to find the right platform and train for their departure to another never-seen-before destination. Others were taking the opportunity for refreshment — troop trains did not usually sport the luxury of a dining car, which, in any event, would not have been frequented on a matelot's rate of pay. The voluntary services were noted for providing a lifeline and were much in evidence wherever the services might congregate as they provided an indeterminate number of cups of tea and pieces of cake, and willing hands to serve them to weary travellers.

Finding a train did not necessarily coincide with finding a seat, and where does one find space to deposit a rolled hammock and a kit-bag? The competition was acute, but a friendly, welcome cry of "in 'ere mate" might, with luck, offer a seat, but more often it represented a small vacant space in the corridor where one stood throughout the journey clutching all that one possessed. At least the views out of the window were attractive, but a visit to the toilet involved a penetrative advance along the corridor and a similar exploit on the way back.

I did not know very much about the town of Rugby except that it had something to do with a game, apparently emanating from a local school, where one player picked up an oval-shaped ball and ran towards a given target while a number of beefy-looking young man did their level best to hurl him to the ground before falling on top of him. I much preferred the game where one kicked a round ball, which seemed to me to have less chance of causing permanent injury and gave the appearance of being marginally friendlier.

I alighted at Rugby station to find I was not alone as I was aware of some of my Royal Arthur shipmates, standing, slightly bewildered, amid a pile of hammocks and kitbags. We were approached by a benign looking Petty Officer who had obviously anticipated our arrival. From the medal ribbons he displayed on his uniform it was obvious that he was a reservist from the First World War and had been recalled or had volunteered for this one — he was to become a father figure to us for the next few weeks.

Our immediate destination was Rugby Technical College, a part of which had become a Royal Naval unit for training prospective Radio Mechanics. In true Naval tradition, it had been "floated" as HMS Shrapnel . . . and we were at least one hundred miles from the sea. The college had no living accommodation and we were billeted with local families, which meant being transported around the neighbourhood and deposited, one by one, into a new family. I thus found myself in a semi-detached, three-bedroom house with an indoor bathroom and two toilets, a far cry from the Spartan facilities of my Paddington home. I had my own room, adequately furnished with a comfortable bed and a real mattress. My shipmates were equally pleased with their allocation.

No time was wasted in getting down to the first part of my training to become a Radio Mechanic, which involved knowledge of electricity and magnetism and the basic principles of Radio, after which I would complete my training elsewhere. Whether I reached that stage would depend upon success in a number of tests throughout the course — failure in any one would see my removal and a draft to the Royal Naval Barracks in Portsmouth. Having learned much of the subject matter in my City and Guilds studies as a Post Office Engineer I did not anticipate much difficulty but I had to guard against the error of over-confidence.

Royal Naval tradition applied as far as it was possible in a close civilian environment, and we were subject to periods of fire watching duties at the college. These entailed an all night vigil, and on these occasions food was left out for us in the college kitchen and we became self-appointed cooks for the evening. On Saturday mornings we were obliged to take part in a cross-country run. Whether this was imposed for the purpose of maintaining our fitness or to prevent a clandestine trip home for the weekend was open to conjecture. Whether such an infringement would constitute breaking ship or merely being absent without leave, I had no intention of putting to the test. To avoid

131

any temptation, I occasionally arranged for my girlfriend Joan to stay in a nearby hotel and so I had no need for such an illicit journey.

Perhaps to my discredit I can remember little else of my stay in Rugby or of the town I must have frequented from time to time, save that it was the home of the General Electricity Company whose presence was advertised by a large sign bearing the initials GEC — no doubt brightly illuminated in happier times. In the other direction the Radio station at Hillmorton was evident by a number of tall aerials, which with the immediate threat of air raids having receded, may have been topped at night with a red light as a warning to our own aircraft. Having a comfortable billet, my washing and feeding included, and a comfortable room in which to study, I was easily satisfied and did not need attraction elsewhere.

The day of our final and conclusive exam was approaching, and like all such occasions what I had not learned was not likely to be assimilated by any period of intense cramming. Sadly, some of our number had already taken the journey to their respective barracks, and this included those across a wide spectrum of educational levels. It had been a short but intense course, wholly technical in nature, and I was fortunate in that my Post Office training had equipped me well, so that I had been able to meet its demands without much difficulty. I had survived, but not without a slight hiccup that could have cost me my place on the course and precipitated an early acquaintance with Royal Navy Barracks at Portsmouth.

On one of my rare weekend leaves I had decided to call on Dad at the ARP office at Paddington Station. It was a hot day, and alighting from the bus I had pushed my hat onto the back of my head to get a little air to a fevered brown. I had often seen this done, but on this occasion I was spotted by the Royal Naval Military Police who, in common with other service police units, regularly patrolled mainline railway stations. I was quietly intercepted, asked for details of my ship and of myself, and sent on my way with a casual injunction to "mind your hat, son". I thought nothing further of the incident until I returned to the college and was required to attend before the commanding officer (a lieutenant), to whom my misdemeanour had obviously been reported — I was well and truly "on the carpet" for what I thought was a minor infringement.

My view of the affair was clearly not shared by my interrogator who lost no time in informing me of what could happen to me; thankfully this did not include being "keel hauled", that is being dragged underneath the boat from port to starboard, a penalty common in the days of sail but now fortunately discontinued. For my sins I was ordered to present my entire kit for inspection by the Petty Officer every morning for a week, a task made easier by the help rendered by my friends but which may have caused more aggravation to the undeserving PO than to myself.

The Day of Judgment arrived and we lounged around the sportsfield attached to the college waiting for the results of our efforts. We had, in any event, been promised a week's leave, after which the successful amongst us would be returning, before proceeding to the next destination, to continue our training. I had arranged for Joan to spend this final weekend with me before we both returned to London for my leave.

Joan was a little younger than me and hailed from South London, being born and bred in Tooting, SW18. She was now living a short distance away in Earlsfield with her parents, and an elder sister who was in the Women's Auxiliary Air Force (WAAF). Her father was a self-employed window cleaner who had, like my own father, seen military service overseas. They were a working class family, like my own, and I got on well with them.

When the results were to be announced I left Joan recumbent in the shade of a tree and hurried with the others into the college. We had all passed! We lost no time in congratulating each other and equally lost no time in departing to the railway station to enjoy a more than welcome break. My seven days at home were not interrupted by the attention of enemy aircraft as the German High Command had apparently abandoned efforts to obtain our capitulation by brute force.

The news from other theatres of war suggested that the tide was beginning to turn in favour of the Allies. In North Africa the German Afrika Corps was in retreat, while on the Eastern front Russian forces had mounted a successful offensive against the German invader. In the air, British and American forces had taken the offensive to the enemy, and bombing raids were mounted by day and by night on a number of German cities.

I was just getting used to the freedom of leave and the comfort of my own bed when the time came for me to return to Rugby. I never liked the moment of taking leave of Mum and Dad and found the occasion emotionally charged, especially as I recognized a similar reaction in both my parents. My brother, with whom I regularly corresponded, had recently left the Naval hospital in Scotland and had gone to sea in HMS Woodcock as a Petty Officer Sick Berth Attendant, which had added an extra poignancy to my departure on this occasion. Dad always liked to see me off at the station whenever he could, and I felt his isolation as he stood alone and watched the train slowly move away. I was always very careful to share as much of my company with them as with my girlfriend.

HMS Ariel

Having returned to Rugby I bade farewell to my civilian hosts, collected my kit, which they had stored for me in their roof space, and joined my shipmates at the college ready for the journey to a new destination where our training to become Radio Mechanics was to continue. We were bound for the (then) small village of Culcheth, close to Warrington in Lancashire and the site of HMS Ariel, another land-locked ship of the Royal Navy. It appeared to be a purpose-built unit and comprised living quarters in the form of an "H"-shaped block containing dormitory accommodation in the sides with toilet and washing facilities in between. Classrooms and a workshop were contained within a secure fenced compound, from which we were forbidden to remove any of our notes — we would, apparently, be dealing with secretly sensitive material. There was also a parade ground (quarterdeck) and a standard, from which, traditionally, flew the White Ensign, but otherwise Naval tradition was a little less intrusive than I had experienced at Royal Arthur.

Radio Aided Direction and Ranging (RADAR) had been used during the Battle of Britain, as evidenced by the tall aerials sited along the East and South Coasts. But it had its limitations and required two or more stations to vector the flight of aircraft to determine the range and position of an enemy target and to monitor its progress. We were to study the latest developments and to understand the basic principles of Radar, the circuits and components necessary to produce High Frequency pulses, and how to set up and maintain the equipment.

I do not intend to bore my reader with any detailed descriptions except to say that I learned about a Kipp Relay, a Push-pull oscillator and a Plan Position Indicator, together with other strange-sounding devices that I cannot now remember. We followed the development of the rotary aerial, that would give all-round vigilance and which together with a combined transmitter/receiver could be fitted into an aircraft so as to provide an air-to-air and air-to-ground facility. It was thereby possible to obtain both range and bearing of any target and was a leap forward in attack capability on the ground and in the air.

Our leisure time was not neglected and there was a large hall that served as dance hall and theatre, and any other activity in which the ship's company might be involved. We were occasionally visited by units from ENSA, a body set up at the beginning of the war, which drew into its fold actors and other entertainers from civilian life and also from members of the three services who showed promise in the field of entertainment. It went under the title of "Entertainments National Services Association" and provided a wide range of entertainment for the services at home and, later, abroad. They did an excellent job, often in difficult or hazardous conditions, although their efforts were sometimes, rather unfairly, referred to as "Every Night Something Awful" — criticism that, in my experience, was not deserved. Nevertheless, there must have been many who were introduced to theatre and music for the first time, and the comedy sessions were a welcome relaxant.

There is one programme that stands out in my memory concerning a two-man team — one called Dobson and the other called Young . . . and both were named Walter. They toured the country in a small car, packed with equipment, and gave illustrated talks on music in many service establishments. They had agreed to give four live broadcasts and HMS Ariel had been selected for the last of these in which they gave an ingenious and entertaining programme in the cause of music. Dobson was the man who did all the talking, while Young put on the records. I remember they introduced the programme by playing records of a baby crying, the beat of African tom-tom drums, Bing Crosby singing and a contribution from a full symphony orchestra — they then informed their audience, "What you have heard is all music". They soon had the assembly appreciating the classical composers by way of Bing Crosby, Vera Lynn (the Forces' Sweetheart) and the latest import from America — Swing! They had been called clowns, but they had a technique that could soon win over the most stubborn audience and make the man in uniform listen to music and then think about it. Sadly they disappeared from the public arena soon after the war and I never heard of them again.

Occasionally we were required to perform an overnight guard duty at what I believe was an airfield a few miles away from HMS Ariel. I never discovered its precise location except that it had a hyphenated name, which looking at my map of the district could have been Newton-le-Willows — I proffer my apologies if I have misrepresented that fair town. The objects of our nightly vigil were a number of old aircraft which, I recall, included a Swordfish and a Walrus, both of which deserve the description of stately gentlemen of Naval airpower.

The Swordfish was a biplane, reputed to have been constructed of canvas and string, and for which reason had become affectionately known as "Old Stringbag". Some were later adapted to accept radar equipment, necessitating the fitting of a bulbous construction under the fuselage that earned it the additional description of "pregnant". Slow moving and said to be able to "turn on a sixpence", it had nevertheless given good service as a torpedo bomber and could claim a number of successes.

The Walrus, too, had a certain oddity in design in that the engine was mounted facing astern and situated behind the pilot's cockpit. Both aircraft were capable of landing and taking off on water with the necessary modification of adding floats. I remember them silhouetted against the evening skyline, a monumental reminder of days when travel was more sedate. They are both now museum pieces in graceful retirement.

The occasion gave me the opportunity of sleeping in a hammock for the first time. We were briefly accommodated in a small hut, sufficient for preparing and eating our food, but it was necessary to sling our hammocks each night for sleeping. Now there is a technique for climbing into a hammock suspended some few feet off the ground that involves swinging up until one is level with the target, and then projecting the body swiftly sideways to land securely in the well of the hammock without having it spin over and depositing one on the floor on the opposite side. One either masters the challenge or sleeps on the floor — I must have had the necessary athleticism because I found this method of sleeping to be most comfortable. In the morning one reverses the operation to give effect to the expression "rolling out of bed", after which it becomes the matter of "lash up and stow" until the next time.

Back on board HMS Ariel (even land-locked sailors can be allowed to stretch their imagination), the course

139

was coming to an end. It had not been all work and no play, and I often joined my friends and ventured into Warrington to explore its entertainment facilities. This invariably meant an early visit to the local fish and chip shop — a common target wherever sailors are to be found ashore — followed by a visit to the cinema, all rounded off by a trip to the nearest public house to "have a jar". This expression seemed to be confined to the North Country, as I never encountered it during my youth — perhaps I had led too sheltered an existence. In any event I was not attracted to it as I found the mere taste of the liquid unpleasant and still do today. I much preferred the product of the West Country apple to that of the Kentish hops.

An alternative to a trek into the local town might be a short walk into the village containing a charming English country pub, which I believe went under the name of "The Labour in Vain" — hopefully not a pronouncement upon my efforts during the past few months.

I had survived, so far, and one last hurdle remained to be mounted which would determine whether I would aspire to the rank of Leading Radio Mechanic (Radar) or take a tumble at the last fence. For our last test we were presented with a variety of components and required to build a simple wireless set — and it had to work first time. My Post Office training had allowed me to become competent in wiring abilities, and I had received a solid grounding in the secrets of Radio during the course, so I felt confident so long as I was able to keep my nerve. I saw the benefits of taking my brother's timely advice and I would no longer have to struggle with the tight jumper and other paraphernalia of "square rig" that would be replaced with a jacket, trousers, a nice white shirt and a peaked cap to top it all. I would, in short, change from "square rig" to "fore and aft" — I never discovered why either should be so described. Bell bottomed trousers had a certain glamour — it was customary to press them horizontally into "seven seas" creases — and I should no longer be the target of the ladies wishing to "touch my collar for luck".

Having presented myself in the workshop I was directed to a table containing a selection of components and a supply of wire; then I was left to my own devices. I deftly manipulated my tools and watched as my masterpiece developed until I was able to present it to my examiner. I now waited with bated breath as he connected the finished product to a battery and loudspeaker while I manipulated the tuning control and slowly increased the volume. The result was, literally, music to my ears as its dulcet tones signalled a success that drew a comment of "Well done . . . now you can take it to pieces again." The variety of sounds that echoed around the room from various other efforts at wireless making indicated that I was not alone in my success. There had been no failures, and we had all surmounted the final hurdle — the long course was finally over and we had earned the right to wear the coiled anchor, known as a killick, on our left sleeve to denote the rank of leading seaman, and thereafter, in Naval slang, to be referred to as a "killick".

It had been an intensive course and we were in no hurry to find pastures new. Our time was now taken up in receiving our new uniforms which took the usual form of a No.1 and No.2 issue, and it was a pleasure to wear what I felt to be a more civilized form of dress. No longer would I be required to wear the sailor's round cap with a "tiddly bow" placed above the left eyebrow, and my skill at ironing would now be exercised on my acquisition of white shirts and black tie.

We were permitted to wear a No.1 suit of another material, so long as it did not infringe regulation dress. This was a privilege often accepted. Doe-skin was a favourite choice of material, but required the services of a bespoke tailor to bring it to fruition, and one who could supply our needs in a relatively short time as our departure from HMS Ariel would not be long delayed. One of our number, a Liverpool lad, said he knew just the man and at the first opportunity three of us ventured into that city and gave an order which, we were promised, would be ready within a week. Our tailor friend was true to his word, and after just one mid-week fitting we emerged a week later with our spoils.

My time was soon taken up sewing new badges on my recent acquisitions, and I took a special delight in the gold wire ones that adorned my doeskin suit. I was now, for all to see, a Leading Radio Mechanic (AR), which I understood to denote Air Radar in contrast to AW (Air Wireless). My port division now changed from Portsmouth to the Fleet Air Arm with a consequent change in my service number which now became

FAA.674233. It was not long before the reason became clear.

We crowded together in excited anticipation as we waited to see where our new postings would take us. I had, some time previously, been invited to express my preference between service at sea or at home, and I had chosen the former — after all, that is why I wanted to join the Senior Service. One by one our names were read out, together with our intended port of call . . . my own name being followed by "Royal Naval Air Station, Twatt". I had no idea where this place was until I heard a small voice alongside me telling me that I was bound for the Orkney Islands. I cannot recall my immediate reaction except that I, a London boy, had been drafted over 700 miles away, which I thought about as far as I could possibly go short of going to sea. Neither did I find any consolation that it also went under the name of HMS Tern; it was still where I would be spending Christmas and the winter months, and I would be unlikely to indulge in an occasional weekend leave unless I learned to fly.

At least I had seven days' leave to enjoy, so I gathered my gear, which now included a green suitcase and a wooden toolbox, and found my way in all haste to the local railway station.

HMS Tern

I remember very little of the journey except that I did not wear my treasured doe-skin outfit, as I declined to subject it to the ravages of humping a hammock and kitbag ctcctcra on and off the rolling stock of the London, Midland and Scottish Railway and then half-way across London. I cannot even remember how I managed to transport such a burden to arrive, thankfully, at my own front door where I received a great welcome and was glad to be home with a cup of real tea and with much news to be exchanged.

It was customary for the Navy to pay my fare whenever I travelled on leave, and in addition I was supplied with an emergency ration card to supplement the rations at home as my parents could not have satisfied the needs of a virile and hungry young man from their meagre allowance. In order to supplement the ration allowance, other foodstuff that was not subject to restriction was available from time to time, and its appearance in a shop was guaranteed to produce a queue of indeterminate length. It was surprising how news spread, and consequently the shop soon exhausted its entire stock in a very short time and the housewife became expert in vigilance every time she went shopping. One such item was "Spam", a product of America, heralded as a substitute for ham and which I found very tasty, although unaware of the exact ingredients.

Another interesting addition to the ration was the appearance of whale meat, which, in general, was approached with a degree of wariness as it had never been considered as a food item for the British palate. On one occasion when I visited my girlfriend's parents her mother had been able to buy some and I had the opportunity of sampling this newfound challenge to my digestion. I did not like it, either in taste or texture, and I sensed the assembled company shared my opinion, which I had suppressed in the interests of courtesy. Whether it would have been improved by an attempt at tenderizing and with the addition of herbs and spices, I did not wait to find out and I have never been tempted to sample it again.

Shopping must have been an onerous task for my mother, as both she and my father did not appear to be as robust as I would have liked. Fortunately my sisters made frequent visits and were a great help and comfort to me. I had been able to see them on my leave and found that they shared my view. Since my brother and I never had the same period of leave, I did not see him once I joined the Navy and we relied on correspondence to keep in touch with events.

All too soon it was necessary to focus my attention on my journey to the outermost region of the British Isles. When the time came to leave, Dad managed to obtain the use of a former ambulance that had been converted into a passenger-carrying vehicle, which took the two of us, together with my considerable baggage, to Euston Station for me to catch a train to the northern most regions of the country. I had already been advised that the train to take was the 10.30a.m. bound for Thurso on the north coast of Scotland. This train was not a scheduled passenger service but was utilized by servicemen and women serving in the Orkney Islands — in Naval slang it was known as the "Jellicoe". During the First World War a similar train, named after Admiral Sir John Jellicoe, who was engaged in the Naval Battle of Jutland, transported coal from the Welsh coalfields to the coal burning ships of the Navy anchored in Scapa Flow. In both wars this sheltered anchorage was used as a base for the British Grand Fleet.

I arrived at the station in good time, knowing the propensity for such trains to become rapidly overcrowded with servicemen and women, and was able to find a seat and stow my gear. Having said my farewell to Dad, I settled down for what I felt was going to be a long journey and for which I had been supplied with ample provisions. The train left promptly at 10.30 and proceeded unhurriedly, with the occasional stop for reasons I did not know except that we did not take any additional passengers aboard — perhaps we were acting as a quasi-goods train in addition to a military passenger service. Sleep evaded most of us in the carriage, lit only by the regulation blue light, and conversation lapsed as we exhausted any further topics of interest.

I do remember stopping at Perth station at two o'clock in the morning, when I, and a few others, took the opportunity to stretch our legs, but any hope of refreshment vanished as we viewed a cold, bleak and deserted station. There was, I believe, a form of buffet somewhere along the train that involved a walk along the corridors strewn with fellow travellers, where one could obtain a "bacon butty", the recipe for which escaped me — it was not a delicacy that was common in the South of England. One of my travelling companions made the journey only to find supplies had been exhausted and the facility closed — I was glad I had taken precautions against the pangs of hunger that some of my fellow passengers must have suffered.

As the train slowly rumbled on I watched as the light of dawn revealed a bleak and barren landscape, which seem to be devoid of any human occupation and which I hoped did not portray a foretaste of my surroundings in the months to come.

Eventual arrival at Thurso saw me once again on alien territory, with my worldly possessions around me, being gently ushered until I found myself on the quayside waiting to board a small tender to take me across the Pentland Firth to the Orkneys. I had been told that the Pentland Firth had the reputation of being the roughest stretch of water around the British Isles, and I now faced the journey in what appeared to be a lightweight vehicle. If I had been born with "sea legs" I was about to put them to the test. As it so happened, I crossed into Scapa Flow on a gentle swell and came alongside a vessel with the name of Dunluce Castle. I believe this had been a former passenger ship, anchored in the middle of the Flow, and was now pressed into service as a half-way stage for those posted to one of the many surrounding islands. Anchored below the companionway with the ship towering above us, I made two journeys to transport my gear, including a hammock and kitbag, hoping I would not drop either into the briny below or lose my footing and follow them in — if this is what having sea legs meant then I was surely testing mine.

147

My ultimate destination of Twatt was on the mainland, and it was necessary to pick up a further tender to take me to Stromness, from whence I hoped I should find transport to deliver me to HMS Tern and journey's end. I was directed to a point "forrard on starboard side", which interpreted meant I should go to the sharp end on the right-hand side of the ship. The wait enabled me to look around at the vast expanse of inland harbour, home of the Grand Fleet in both World Wars. It was here, in the earliest days of the war, that a German U-Boat had been able to penetrate one of the entrances to the harbour and torpedo the battleship HMS Royal Oak with the loss of most of its crew. As a result barriers were hastily constructed to link Lambs Holm, Glimps Holm and Burray with the mainland, to close three of the entrances to the Flow. They became known as the Churchill Barriers, and a main road was subsequently built upon them to seal their permanency.

The question of visibility was one that arose on many occasions. I had been told that the whole of my present panorama was often enshrouded in a thick fog and it was not unusual to lose sight of one's neighbour for some time. The jest of a Scotch mist might not be appreciated in these parts.

When my "taxi" arrived I had the dubious pleasure of making a return journey, with my entire gear, down another companionway onto an equally small tender, but after two or three journeys I accomplished the mission without mishap. I eventually reached my destination more than one whole day since leaving home and a new experience was about to begin.

148

The scene with which I was now presented was most foreboding. I had left the bustle of West London and the greenery of the London Park, and now looked out upon a barren, open landscape with not a tree to be seen in any direction. I should not have been surprised if an outstretched hand and a casual "Doctor Livingstone I Presume" had welcomed my arrival, such was the effect upon this young London boy. I pondered upon the fact that I could be nearer to occupied Norway than to my own fireside back home, and judging by the temperature neither could I be far from the Arctic Circle. I now understood the purpose of my issue of heavy woollen underwear, which featured a pair of long pants and a vest that together provided protection from the neck to the toes — they were not to be viewed as articles of elegance and could be rather itchy to the skin. Despite the cold, I could not bring myself to wear them, and later I took them home where they were unpicked and the wool was used to produce a more acceptable form of clothing.

I still had a little further to go and was taken to a group of Nissen huts situated on the edge of the airfield, which was to be my home for the foreseeable future. It went under the name of "Downatown" and took on the semblance of some remote outpost of the Empire. It was a self-contained unit with sleeping quarters, ablutions (toilet facilities, commonly called "the heads"), and a galley and mess deck where the inner man was catered for. The Nissen hut was a tunnel-shaped hut of corrugated iron with a cement floor and named after PN Nissen, the British Engineer responsible for its design in 1930. The building that served as sleeping quarters had beds along both sides and was heated by a central stove with a chimney through the roof.

Welcomed in, I found a spare bed and deposited my gear for what I hoped would be the last time for some time. It was here that I finally met my fellow Radio Mechanics and other technical grades who were to become my shipmates. The cooks and other personnel occupied another Nissen hut, and each hut was responsible for maintaining its own cleanliness with a routine that required collective responsibility — and woe betide anyone who let the stove go out for want of a knob or two of coal. I had found a new home with a ready-made family in surroundings that could hardly be called salubrious, and it would be essential that we all got on, with the minimum of friction between us. One thing I had learned during my short time in the Navy was that there was another world beyond the confines of a London Borough, and there were accents and temperaments that had to be understood and tolerated.

I quickly made friends with a young lad, named Banks, who hailed from the North East of England. When he enquired where I came from, I replied "Paddnton" in the London vernacular, which caused a mild ripple of amusement. I realized I had just christened myself with the name by which I was to be known, and we immediately became buddies — or "oppos" (opposite numbers) in Naval terminology. I was familiar with the description of "Taffy" for a Welshman, and to the Scots answering to the name of

"Jock", so I felt my own nickname at least had an air of originality.

Our working quarters were situated a further mile away and seemed even more remote, necessitating a walk back and forth for meals twice every day. This was no hardship to the fit and healthy specimens we thought we were . . . but the winter was yet to come! "Workshops", as this venue was known, consisted of a large wooden structure divided into two rooms, the largest of which was to serve as our daily workshop. The officer in charge of the unit used the smaller room, heated by an open fire and also containing a single bed, the use of which soon became apparent.

The larger room, where we kept our tools, was heated by a single stove which was kept alight 24 hours each day as our duties occasioned staying overnight in our isolated outpost — the need for the bed in the smaller room was now apparent. In addition to maintaining warmth in the workshop, the fire in the officer's accommodation had to be cleared and re-lit each day ready for his arrival. It nevertheless had its compensations, for the early mornings often featured a dawn such as I have never witnessed before. I often stood in awe at the shades of turquoise and pink that preceded the arrival of the sun and which the fog-bound skies of London could never produce. It was a humbling experience and the walk back for breakfast seemed all the more enjoyable.

The real reason for our being in this small deserted patch of the Orkneys was soon to become apparent. A short walk from the workshop, and hidden from view, was a large area given over to the storage of a number of aircraft, lined up in military order. These included a number of Barracudas, which were, I believe, two-seater dual-purpose machines, and the larger Boston which may have undertaken reconnaissance work. They had been put into temporary retirement, having given way to the advanced technology of aircraft engineering and the arrival of American machines. Nevertheless they required regular maintenance and their radar facilities had to be constantly monitored. Both aircraft must have played their part in the earlier surveillance of the North Atlantic in case the German Navy might have been tempted to break out from its long restriction in the port of Bremen to make inroads into our shipping lanes and beyond. But with the war going well on all fronts this possibility no longer appeared to be an immediate threat.

In the Middle East, Italy had surrendered, the dictator Mussolini had been deposed and German forces left to carry on any resistance to the advancing Allied forces. In Russia, the German forces were in retreat and the bitter winter was about to close in on them. At home, the last of the German Naval threat had been successfully dealt with in the sinking of the battleship Scharnhorst, whilst making a dash for the port of Brest in France, together with an attack upon the Tirpitz, which left it damaged and marooned in port to take no further part in the war.

We took the maintenance duties in turns; "Banksie" and I worked together but it was a cold undertaking. We were both equipped in thick Duffle coats, together with sturdy knee-length boots, and with the weather threatening snow, they were to be invaluable, especially for the long walk back to the mess deck at mealtimes. It was necessary that a supply of electricity was available on each aeroplane, which would normally have been obtained from its own battery, but this was not available and must have been disconnected, so we had to resort to the use of a contraption called a "petro-electric" set. This was effectively a dynamo driven by a petrol engine that needed cranking with a starting handle, as was the practice with the earliest motorcar. This was an energetic exercise in that the engine generally disliked being aroused from its slumbers and took some time and effort to make it spark into life — even more so when the weather was cold. Once success had been achieved it was just a question of plugging it into an appropriate place on the aircraft. Since this machine was used on other maintenance work, it was rarely found conveniently close to where we wanted it, and more often incurred a pedestrian search to find the nearest one . . . and one that worked.

Each aircraft was fitted with a small Radar set and a screen providing the means for observation over a wide field; and which was required to be in an instant state of readiness. Any equipment in need of attention was dealt with in the workshop and any adjustment or repair carried out. We were not overworked and it could be a monotonous existence in which we looked forward to mealtimes and a welcome walk back to the mess and fresh faces to see and talk to. We divided our days into

153

working shifts — we were no longer subject to the repetitive sound of tannoyed instructions, and if we had been I doubt that we could have heard any in our rather remote enclosure . . . but nevertheless time seemed to pass all too slowly.

I confess I was disappointed that I had so little to occupy my time as I had hoped that I would be attached to a squadron and become part of the bustle of a busy air station. But it was not to be and so I made use of my leisure time by exploring the local surroundings of wide-open spaces with a small croft dotted here and there, each struggling to find a living with a few farm animals and chickens running free range around. The Orkney Islands, of which there are many, were reputed to have been part of Scotland many thousands of years ago but a strong link still existed with the Viking tradition. Old Norse names predominated and the people were a blend of Norse and Scots; I found them very friendly, hardworking and a rugged race in their sturdy stone crofts with thick walls built to withstand the rigours of the near arctic conditions that prevailed in the winter.

On one of my excursions I stopped to talk to a local inhabitant who asked me if I would like a half-dozen new laid eggs. My mind immediately turned to Mum and Dad and I visualized them trying to prepare a tasty meal of dried egg of indeterminate age from a cardboard packet occasionally available from the shops. I graciously accepted the offer with the intention of sending them home and on my return I proceeded to wrap each one individually in plenty of newspaper and made a neat parcel that I hoped would survive the rigours of the British postal service. I never heard whether my effort ever reached my parents or, if it had done so, in what condition it arrived. Perhaps their silence was intended to spare my embarrassment, but I did not enquire when next I visited home and I never knew the ultimate fate of my well-meant gift. On reflection, perhaps I was a little naïve and now console myself that it is the thought and not the deed that matters.

Transport was regularly provided for those wishing to have a "run ashore" which meant, in reality, a 15-mile journey to Kirkwall, the administrative capital of the Orkney Islands. The main feature of this small town lay in its splendid cathedral of St Magnus, which was the only really dominant feature. I was an infrequent visitor to Kirkwall and have little recollection of what entertainment was available, although I do recall the hospitality of the people of the town and especially the facilities for a cup of tea and a piece of cake provided by the local Kirk (Church) groups — they were well accustomed to the presence of the Senior Service amongst them and made us welcome.

For those who were able to make the journey, a visit to the Italian Chapel on Lamb Holm was a rewarding event. It was, I believe, a Nissen hut provided for the benefit of Italian prisoners of war who took it upon themselves to decorate the inside in the Italian style; they produced a building of intense beauty — Michelangelo would have applauded their efforts.

Christmas came and went without making any lasting impression upon my memory. It was a tradition in the Royal Navy that the Christmas meal for the men of the lower deck was served by the officers, but I have no recall of being a recipient of this privilege or any other jollification to mark the festive occasion. Neither do I remember whether any of my shipmates were granted any leave — I certainly was not and, in any event, having arrived a matter of weeks previously I had no wish to endure the return journey for the sake of a couple of days at home.

There was, in the principal part of the camp, a building set aside for entertainment that was used when the travelling units from ENSA put on a show for our benefit. On one occasion our entertainment was provided by two young comedians who became popular favourites after the war, as indeed did many others who had "cut their teeth" before the critical audiences of service personnel. Whatever their talent, they provided a welcome break from a monotonous routine and their visits always attracted a large audience.

With the advent of a new year came a change in the weather. I had often heard tales of the "frozen north", and until now Orkney and Shetland had been nothing more than a mention in the days when the weather and shipping forecast was a regular feature on the wireless. I had, when much younger, enjoyed the rare occasion of playing snowballs in the street, but I was not prepared for the weather conditions that greeted the New Year. Although the amount of snow made walking a difficult exercise, an additional hazard was to be found in the trenches that had been excavated around the perimeters of the airfield to act as a deterrent to the landing of enemy aircraft and which rapidly filled with snow. To the unwary a sudden descent up to one's knees came as a bit of a shock that was rarely repeated.

But it was the wind that caught my attention and more often my breath. It came straight from the Arctic, unhindered across a flat barren landscape, and I came to realize why there was an absence of trees on the island; saplings could not have survived the onslaught. I do not know how far up the Beaufort scale it registered, but I have never before met the occasion to lean forward at an angle of 45° to avoid been blown backwards off my feet or to move at anything but a run with a wind astern. The expression that "it could be worse at sea" did little for my sea-going ambition. I have never since that time experienced such conditions and, much later, when in conversation the subject of the windy weather is raised, I permit myself a dry smile knowing that I have known it to be worse.

Despite the weather, we were not stopped from working and our nightly vigils came along with unwelcome regularity, but even then I was afforded the compensation of a colourful dawn and on one occasion I am sure I saw, late one evening, a glimpse of the Northern Lights. My girlfriend was a telephone operator in the War Office in London and she too had the doubtful pleasure of night duty and, if I was similarly engaged, she was able to telephone me and we exchanged all the up to date news. Whether we were infringing any of the laws relating to the Defence of the

Realm I do not know, but if we did I would plead it was an aid to our morale.

The solace of Winter was knowing that Spring could not be far behind; a time when I might be able to explore the islands a little more. But it was not to be. In late March I received a telegram to tell me that Mum was extremely unwell and, although it did not suggest I should return home, I felt obliged to inform the Lieutenant in charge of the unit. He suggested I should apply for a short period of leave on compassionate grounds and immediately took the necessary steps for me to be given four clear days at home with immediate effect. I hastily packed a few clothes, secured the rest of my gear on my bed and departed for the long journey — a complete reversal of the one I had undertaken only a few months earlier.

Mum had often suffered from severe headaches and the doctor had suggested it was Neuralgia, but this attack had caused sufficient concern, as her sight appeared to be impaired. There was little I could do and my sisters had taken control of the situation. My brother was, as far as we knew, somewhere on board ship, and since he was in no position to take any action, he had not been informed. I was assured that everything was under control and I could only give support and comfort for the next few days.

HMS Ariel Revisited

Before I was due to return I received instruction to proceed to HMS Ariel where I had qualified only a few months before. How this order had been delivered I cannot remember, except that the service of the Police was often used in such circumstances, but whatever, I was in no doubt that it was genuine. In consequence, at the end of my short leave I found myself back at Ariel — but the bulk of my gear was still reclining on my bed in a Nissen hut in the Orkney Islands. Fortunately I had enough clothes in my case to last me for a few days, but how long would it take for the rest of my belongings to join them? If ever! I harboured a faint hope that I might yet find my way back and explore the Islands more — I had even contemplated the possibility of hiring a bicycle for the purpose ... given fair weather it was good cycling country.

None of my new shipmates at Ariel had any idea why we had been summoned, and, as expected, rumour joined forces with guesswork and provided a subject of conversation. The course of the war was going well and the general clamour, both at home and from our Russian allies, was for a second front to be mounted in Europe, and it was generally thought that our summons might be connected in some way. The reason finally became apparent when we all assembled together to be informed that we had been recalled for the purpose of instruction in the latest developments in Radar. It was also necessary to become acquainted with American technology for which we might become responsible — and so I went back into the schoolroom but without the apprehension that had attended my previous visit.

The American equipment came with a surprise — it did not appear to be easily repaired, if at all. We had been used to the multi-coloured wiring of the British version which enabled the route of the wiring to be determined from origin to destination and which assisted in any repair. The American product contained all-white wiring encased in a tight former and provided no facility for repair. The American policy was, apparently, one of "if it works, leave it alone" and "if it doesn't, replace it and throw the old one away". I decided it might make my job easier but it offended my sense of economy and value.

There had been considerable advances in the system that we had come to recognize as Radar, and in the process of updating our technical knowledge of the latest developments we spent a few weeks at HMS Collingwood, another land-locked arm of the Navy in Portsmouth. It was a crowded "ship" but for our purposes it only served as a hotel providing "bed and breakfast and an evening meal". I never discovered the delights enjoyed by the other inhabitants except that discipline appeared to be high on the daily agenda and there was a plethora of Chief Petty Officers waiting to pounce upon the unwary matelot who might be seen with his hands in his pockets or cap not affixed to his head in the regulation manner. They seemed to appear, as if from nowhere, and leading rates, like myself, were not immune.

Our ultimate destination was a daily visit to HMS Excellent, otherwise known as Whale Island, that was the venue of the Royal Naval Gunnery School. It was created in the eighteenth century when excavations were carried out in the harbour of Portsmouth to form an anchorage for ships of the Royal Navy and from which the present Naval base developed. The spoils were deposited on one side and left in what became a small island, which some time later was linked to the mainland by a causeway and developed as a school for the purpose of teaching the art of gunnery in what were then sailing ships of the line carrying a broadside of 60 or even 100 guns, each one supporting a team of six gunners.

Whale Island became synonymous with discipline in teaching the team work required to make an efficient gun crew, and competition between the three divisions of Chatham, Portsmouth and Devonport (Plymouth) later developed and became a feature at the Royal Tournament, an annual event held in London, and which focused upon the prowess of each of the three services in turn each year. My own division of the Fleet Air Arm joined later when Chatham was closed down.

It is interesting to note that much Naval slang originated from the days when Royal Navy ships were propelled by sail and the guns manhandled into position in preparation for battle. There was an expression which I frequently met during my time when I was encouraged to team effort by being exhorted to "two six — heave ho". This phrase is reputed to have an origin in the days of "Heart of Oak', when the gun crews consisted of eight men, numbered one to eight — four on each side of a cannon. After it had been fired it recoiled back a few feet and was then reloaded, and upon completion the gun captain shouted "two — six heave" whereupon numbers two and six heaved on the lines and pulled the cannon back into its firing position. The cannons were extremely heavy and the instruction was as much an order as a warning for the rest of the team to stand clear to avoid injury.

One of the developments in Radar involved the introduction of an exceptionally high frequency set which we knew as the 277, and which provided an improvement in the accuracy essential in gunnery control — it was said to be able to identify the splash of a shell around the target and to greatly assist the task of gun laying. It utilized a new element called a Magnetron, technically described as an "electron tube for amplifying or generating microwaves, with the flow of electrons controlled by an external magnetic field" — an ideal component for the purpose of accurate Radar. It had one drawback in that it could not be worked upon while it was generating, for its radiation was dangerous and therefore the equipment was designed to switch off the power supply immediately it was opened. It was rumoured that an article of food placed within the compartment would be heated by the effect of the magnetron's characteristics, and although I never put this to the test it is significant that, 60 years later, my wife is, at this moment, preparing a meal using our microwave oven, which has now become a feature of nearly every household although care still has to be exercised in its use and it is designed to function only when the door is closed.

I enjoyed my few weeks at Collingwood, not least because it was the nearest I had ever been to my home and I was able to take advantage of a "Friday while" — a short, authorized weekend leave lasting from midday on Friday until early Monday morning. I made the most of these precious few hours and tried to return as close to the Monday deadline as possible. This meant that I often found myself, in the early hours, in the company of many like-minded shipmates, on the platform of Waterloo station waiting for the departure of what was known as "the milk train" which took a slow ponderous journey with many stops but which arrived in time for us to report our arrival and to collect our station cards before our time expired — it was worth the effort.

The course was nearing conclusion but there was one more event to occupy my attention. I awoke one morning to the sound of aircraft, and on looking out of the window, as far as the eye could see, there was a host of Allied aircraft with three white stripes painted on the side, each towing a glider also bearing three white stripes. They came in an endless stream, and it did not take much imagination to realize that a raid of some significance was in progress. The news soon broke that the much-awaited invasion of Europe was in progress with the landing of Allied troops on five separate beaches on the Normandy coast, supported by the ships of the Royal Navy and planes of the Allied Air Forces. It was to be a bloody battle but signified a turning point in the war — news that was destined to overshadow even our successes in the Italian campaign.

The course concluded, I had expected to return to the Orkneys — I had by now received the return of my

belongings that I had abandoned a few weeks earlier —
but I was destined elsewhere. Once again I arrived on
the doorstep of home, fully laden with hammock,
kitbag and a suitcase, not to mention my wooden
toolbox.

My return home coincided with the renewal of air
attacks on the capital city by a new weapon in the form
of a pilotless aircraft. It contained explosives and flew
until its engines cut out, at which point it went into a
steep dive and exploded on impact. It was the
"Vergeltungs-waffen", German for reprisal weapon, and
being the first of its kind earned the further title of V.1.
It became known as the "Doodlebug" or "Buzz-bomb",
and it could be launched in any weather, day or night.
It was designed to strike terror into the hearts of the
population, and, as soon as the engine stopped, it could
be seen turning into a near vertical dive toward the
ground. If I heard one I would stop, and if it was
coming in my direction I would view it with some
apprehension until it passed over. I would then wait for
it to cut out and count, and from the subsequent
explosion I knew it had landed — but not where! But
they were slow moving and a target for our planes, and
many were destroyed before reaching London.
However, those that succeeded caused considerable
damage and much loss of life.

Despite this, the V.1s seemed to have little effect on
the servicemen and women who frequented the West
End of London with its attractions for service
personnel. Joan and I often spent part of my leave at
one of the servicemen's clubs where we could dance or

just listen to the music. The American Big Bands were particularly popular.

HMS Nighthawk

With my leave over my destination was the Royal Naval Air Station at Drem, a small village south of Edinburgh, in East Lothian, Scotland — another dry-land ship that, true to tradition, bore the name of HMS Nighthawk. It had been an RAF station and was now transferred on loan to meet requirements in the Rosyth area. This involved the formation of a night fighter squadron and the facilities required; Drem was commissioned as HMS Nighthawk and was returned to the RAF in 1946. Once again I was to be in no danger of getting my feet wet, even more so when I learned that I was expected at a Radar unit in the small village of Cockburnspath (pronounced Co'burnspath) and that transport would be made available to carry me the short distance south.

The unit at "Co-Path" was a small one alongside the main London to Edinburgh road (A1), and contained a number of wooden buildings that stretched from the road back to a small sunken lane beyond. It provided a totally independent existence for about 20 ratings, from ordinary seamen to Petty Officer, and included our own cook and galley, with provisions being delivered regularly from the air station at Drem. Three Officers were billeted in a hotel in the village, and I only met them when we were on duty elsewhere. I shared the last small building, close to the lane, with another Radio

165

Mechanic named Danny Edge and we became "oppos" together — he was responsible for the maintenance of the Radio communication unit whilst I, and the Petty Officer, took care of the Radar.

The purpose of my being there was a Radar station situated a short distance away on the edge of a small cliff overlooking the North Sea. It was a plotting station and was being used to train Fleet Air Arm pilots in guided approach to a target using the principle of Radar. We had two Radar screens and ancillary equipment, together with plotting tables upon which the movement of aircraft under our control and guidance would be plotted. Outside on the cliff top stood a large aerial array mounted on a turntable, which when in use rotated through 360° to provide an all round Radar search, giving both range and bearing on the console screens, before which trained officers directed the aircraft by Radio link. The radio equipment for this was situated further down the lane where my "oppo", Danny, was in charge. My job as a Radar mechanic was to maintain the equipment in accurate working order.

Off shore, some 14-miles away, was the small bird sanctuary of Bass Rock, and it was upon this that we trained our sets to check and maintain their accuracy. We worked both by day and night, and I found the experience interesting, especially when I watched the Radar "blips" on the screen translated into the movement of aircraft on the plotting table. At last I felt that I was engaged in a worthwhile occupation.

A large area of grass surrounded the building. I have never seen so many rabbit holes, and I would stand and watch the wildlife scurrying to and fro seemingly indifferent to my presence. I was reminded of the times when I had watched Mum prepare a rabbit for the pot until, eventually, I had become adept at this skill and taken over the chore. Dad occasionally came home carrying a brace of rabbits that he had been given by one of the staff at some country station where his train had stopped during the day. I could then be seen in the stone-floored scullery skinning and preparing them for dinner — I got sixpence for each skin from a local factory that I passed on the way to school.

The Radar site was in a secured area, and as the security guard was also a trained gamekeeper he taught me how to make and lay snares that would catch rabbits in a humane manner. I had limited success, but when I was successful I took one or two to the cook in the galley. Although I offered my assistance in preparation of the rabbits, he did not always receive them with an excess of enthusiasm . . . but it did serve to vary our diet from time to time. He generally followed with deep fried jam sandwiches in batter, a favourite when all inspiration had failed.

Back at our quarters, although we enjoyed a relaxed atmosphere and were a closely-knit team, it was important to maintain some form of traditional discipline and the essential Naval routines had to be adhered to. We were each responsible for keeping our own quarters clean and tidy and ourselves clean and neatly dressed. As Leading Hands, the Radio

Mechanics were responsible for ensuring that this was done throughout the camp. Time not spent on our duties elsewhere was partly spent in "make do and mend", or in "dhobying" our washing which readily dried on the perimeter fence. Such efforts were quickly removed before the Commanding Officer, a Lieutenant-Commander, appeared on his weekly round of inspection.

For our relaxation and pleasure we could venture into Dunbar, a coastal town about eight miles north, or a longer journey over the border into Berwick-upon-Tweed. The unit had its own transport and it was used for such "runs ashore" and in maintaining our link with the air station at Drem, of which we were an outlying unit. The accommodation that Danny Edge and I shared was close to the little lane at the rear of the camp and we often slipped quietly away to visit a small rocky cove or, in the other direction, to the main road and a conveniently placed café where we made the acquaintance of Annie, a charming young lady who supplied us with tea and homemade cakes. Perhaps our absence was assumed to be due to pressing matters at the Radar site!

Danny was a keen exponent of the martial art of Ju Jitsu, a form of Japanese unarmed combat, which involves throwing one's opponent to the ground using a minimum of force. He offered to teach me a few of the moves, and for this purpose we took the mattresses from our beds (Yes, these were supplied and our hammocks thus remained lashed up and stowed!) and placed them on the ground in an adjoining grassy field.

168

I succeeded in executing some of the throws to his satisfaction, but I never managed, having been catapulted over his shoulder, to master the art of falling gracefully; I invariably landed in a breath-destroying heap, grateful that I had fallen on something soft instead of the hard ground.

It was reasonable to suppose that my stay in Co'Path would last throughout the summer, and so on my next leave I returned with my bicycle and cycling attire and spent many hours of off-duty leisure exploring the countryside north of the border. My immediate superiors had no objection to my excursions, but I did attract some ribald comment from my shipmates when I went to and fro dressed in shorts, white jacket and cycling shoes. However, I enjoyed myself and the shorts came in useful when we formed a football team to play a local village side. For the record books, we lost by seven goals to one, but I did have the honour of scoring our solitary reply, which redeemed me in the eyes of my critics.

It was to be the longest time that I had served in any one ship and as time went on the Allies' successes elsewhere began to suggest that the war in Europe might be drawing to a close. The capture of the French ports had effectively brought an end to the U-Boat threat to our shipping, and our forces had established superiority both on the ground and in the air. It was therefore not surprising that the focus of attention moved from Europe to the Far East where American forces had taken the initiative with the bombing of Japan and the invasion of the Philippines.

On a personal note, the time I had served as a Leading Radio Mechanic qualified me for promotion, and I was summoned before the Captain at RNAS Drem to be made up to Petty Officer. In any other circumstances this would have entitled me to move into the Petty Officer's mess, but since our small establishment did not afford this luxury I stayed, quite happily, in my little hut at Co'Path. However, one of the perquisites of such advancement entitled me to a daily issue of undiluted rum, commonly called "neaters", and I decided to take advantage of the privilege. I renewed my needlework skills to sew new badges on all my items of uniform — I now proudly displayed the crossed anchors topped by a crown, the traditional badge of a Petty Officer. Dad now had two Petty Officers in the family.

Although the war appeared to be coming to a timely end something sinister appeared on the scene. Hitler began sending over rockets. They came with a silent approach and with no warning of their presence; they could not be seen or heard until they landed with a ton of high explosive, which created considerable damage and loss of life. They were capable of destruction over a wider area than we had, so far, experienced. Fortunately their impact on the war was short-lived when their launch sites in Holland were discovered and destroyed. What effect they might have had on morale if they had been delivered earlier in the war must remain a matter of conjecture — thankfully, they never developed into the status of a secret weapon. By the time I came home on leave in December the threat had ceased to exist and I had my first Christmas with the family since I joined the Navy.

I found that Mum had been having problems with her eyes and had been receiving medical attention. Both she and Dad were spending the holiday with my eldest sister, Dorrie, who had recently moved to Potters Bar in Hertfordshire. On the journey, by train from Co'Burnspath, we were delayed outside the station at Potters Bar, and I felt the frustration of having to travel on to Kings Cross only to take another train back to within a few yards of where I had sat so impatiently. I realised that Dad had been struggling to combine the responsibilities of looking after Mum and his work at Paddington Station and, in common with my sisters, believed the time had arrived when he should formally retire. I was relieved when they agreed to take turns in looking after my two parents, and after a quiet Christmas I returned for the New Year in Scotland. The entry into 1945 was equally quiet, and although the Scots are renowned for their celebration of "Hogmanay" I saw little evidence of it and would have welcomed the diversion of the skirl of the bagpipes and the swirl of the kilt — I have since developed a soft spot for the braw race from whom I received much hospitality.

Events continued to move quickly on all the war fronts, especially in the Far East where the conflict would continue after the defeat of Germany. It was about this time that we received information that the Navy was developing a number of mobile air units in readiness for the Japanese campaign in the Philippine Islands and beyond and which would contain all the necessary elements of an operational Naval Air Station. They were known as Mobile Operational Naval Air Bases — MONABS for short, and numbers one and two had, reputedly, already departed. The campaign so far had involved large air and sea movements involving the use of Aircraft Carriers, so it was a reasonable development, but whether this was unsupported rumour or just wishful thinking there was no way of knowing. In any event our operational work at the Radar unit had lessened of late and it was not surprising that we were soon to move.

HMS Goldcrest

We moved as a unit, leaving the Radar site to whatever fate the powers that be deferred. Before our occupation, it had been in the control of the Royal Air Force, which accounted for the Security Guard being Air Force personnel. I turned the key in the lock for the last time, said farewell to my rabbit companions and turned my back on many months of a happy association.

Our new destination was to be Wales, and nearly as far west as one could venture in the principality at a place named Dale. A study of the map revealed that, once again, I should be in sight of the sea — my eagerness for life afloat being overlooked by those who could, with the stroke of the pen, have satisfied my enthusiasm for a life on the ocean wave . . . I was again a dry land sailor and I was not pleased. It was, however, within reach of Milford Haven and Pembroke Dock and I still hoped that some passing ship might be in need of my services. In the meantime it was "two-six on the wagon" as we loaded our gear on to a five-ton lorry for the journey to Edinburgh and thence by train to Kings Cross in London. The final part of the journey was to be from Paddington Station, to which we proceeded to find we had a two-hour wait before onward passage.

I knew that Mother had recently been admitted to Western Ophthalmic Eye hospital, which was only a short bus ride away. I explained this to the Officer in Charge and requested to be allowed to visit. He agreed, but with the direst warnings of what might happen to me if I failed to return in time to catch our next train. I found my mother in a room of her own, sitting up in bed with both eyes bandaged, and I realized she could not see me but had recognized me by my voice — she was surprised and happy. I explained the circumstances that led to my visit and was able to spend some time with her and tell her all my news.

When I enquired of the doctor what had taken place I immediately realized my mother had seen me for the last time.

It was, without doubt, the most poignant moment of my life. For the rest of my life I shall admire her courage and fortitude in meeting such a disability and I never heard her once complain. Both she and Dad set an example that I would find hard to follow. I returned to Paddington somewhat subdued, but grateful for my temporary release knowing that the Lieutenant had taken a calculated risk.

We were met at the station at Haverfordwest by the usual vehicle bearing the imposing letters RN on the side. This took us and our gear along country roads at what seemed like breakneck speed — five-ton lorries were not designed for passenger comfort and the driver seemed oblivious to his human cargo. When a large sign emblazoned *HMS Goldcrest* greeted our arrival the adage that it was better to arrive than to travel was never more true.

A cursory glance at our surroundings revealed what seemed to be a large complex. I had hitherto been accustomed to an existence in peripheral isolation in the Orkneys and in Scotland, but first impressions did not suggest that my present whereabouts were to earn such a description. I learned from later enquiries that the small village of Dale stood on the Dale Peninsula, a part of the principality of Wales which had the reputation of being one of the windiest places in Britain with gusts in excess of 100 miles an hour. To soften the blow, my informant hastened to add that it was also one of the sunniest — perhaps this was the nearest I should get to the Atlantic Ocean or the Mediterranean!

We were by no means the first arrivals. It became clear that most of the various grades of the Navy were already established and I was soon rubbing shoulders, as it were, with Electricians, Motor Mechanics, Signalmen and Telegraphists, and together we represented a complete Naval unit. I shared accommodation in the Petty Officers' Mess in the now familiar Nissen hut; it was comfortable, and I soon felt at ease and began to make new friends. We had our own bar which we managed ourselves in accordance with a strict set of rules, and I no longer had to stand in a long queue at mealtimes — in fact life was altogether more relaxed. A Petty Officers' mess is run on disciplined lines with rules and a conduct of behaviour that is accepted by everyone as being for the common good. Chief Petty Officers are respected and ensure that the rules of the mess are enforced when necessary, and to them is given the last word in most matters.

Elsewhere in the camp was the "NAAFI", a facility provided by the Navy, Army and Air Force Institute for the benefit of those in the armed forces and established wherever there was a large concentration of military personnel. It was here that one could relax with a mug of tea and a wad of cake, although the tea was often the target of some rude remarks — if one believed all that one heard Naafi tea was a beverage to be strictly avoided. The criticism was, in my view, not always deserved but often repeated with a sense of humour attached. In many instances the tea bar also contained a shop where one could buy the domestic essentials of soap, toothpaste and writing paper.

As we were a self contained Radar unit we had been assigned to a part of the camp that suggested that it might have been used earlier in the war as an RDF station manned by the Royal Air Force, as it contained all the elements necessary for the plotting of the movements of enemy aircraft. It featured a large plotting room complete with maps of the surrounding area and a gallery from which operations were controlled. There was evidence of an internal communication system connected to a complex network of electrical relays similar to those I had seen on telephone installations, except that it did not seem to be working. I could not find any technical information or circuit diagrams and, in spite of my enquiries to the local Post Office Engineering Department, precise details of how it worked remained a close secret. Neither could I find any Radar equipment, which led me to believe that the facility had been abandoned and that some of the essential components had been removed.

I had nothing worthwhile upon which to focus my attention, and although other members of our group had been found useful work elsewhere, the Radio Mechanics had little to occupy the long day. However, a few words to my shipmates in the PO's mess and they soon found work for our idle hands, but with the war in Europe approaching its end with the suicide of the German Chancellor in his bunker, I could be forgiven for feeling somewhat surplus to requirement in the immediate future. This was to be emphasized when on 7th May 1945 Germany surrendered unconditionally and the following day was celebrated as Victory in Europe Day.

My attention was now firmly fixed upon that other struggle on the far side of the world. I pondered upon whether there was any truth in the rumours relating to the formation of MONABS or was I guilty of wishful thinking. We were close to the deep-sea port of Milford Haven and I consoled myself that it would be an appropriate port of embarkation and therefore some logical reason why I should be encapsulated in a cocoon in a remote part of West Wales.

Throughout the war we had been fortified with a song that began, "When the lights come on all over the world", presented frequently as a morale booster accompanied by another that promised "There'll be bluebirds over the white cliffs of Dover". The lights had indeed returned, to Europe at least, but as for the bluebirds, I do not believe even the most ardent ornithologist expected such a visitation to these shores. But for me, I felt that somehow the war had passed me by. With the war in the Atlantic having been won, my brother George had departed from HMS Woodcock and been drafted to the Hospital Ship HMS Vita, which I suspected was now en route for the Far East. The chances of following him seemed remote in spite of the continuing stories that suggested that I should follow in the fullness of time.

The Royal Navy, before the war, had put its belief in the battleship as the only way to indulge in war at sea and saw little purpose in the aircraft carrier. Nevertheless, in spite of some opposition, the Ark Royal, in 1937, became the first such ship to be launched and set the standard with its portable means of attack from the air, although it lacked the added advantage of having Radar. The United States of America soon followed and proved, in the battle of Midway, the value of numbers of carriers operating in unison by defeating a large Japanese force and thereby establishing a Naval superiority in the Pacific. Now with the added protection that Radar provided, the

Fleet Air Arm had come into its own and I had high hopes that I might yet become involved. The battles in the Pacific Ocean had seen the emergence of the aircraft carrier as a principle weapon of attack.

Meanwhile I continued the occasional runs ashore to Haverfordwest, jolted and jostled in the back of the "fivetonner", but with headlights now blazing our driver was able to make it a less hair-raising adventure. The return of street lighting after six years darkness was a further reminder of the end of hostilities in my part of the world, and even the cinema, a frequent venue on these occasions, now bade welcome with a blaze of light. The subsequent meal of fish and chips also took on a celebratory flavour.

Having little else to occupy me, I welcomed the opportunity for a few days at home where I was able to help lend a hand to Dad, who was coping remarkably well in looking after Mum. London appeared to be making a supreme effort to return to some semblance of normality and in the streets the trappings of war lay abandoned only to serve as a reminder of six years of conflict. The Air Raid shelters became the habitat of dogs and dust, the ARP offices were empty, save for the charts on the wall and the stirrup pump in the corner, while the water in the Emergency Supply tank supported a film of dust and anything else that would float. There were areas of desolation where large numbers of the capital's population once had their homes, barren except for colonies of wild flowers that had sprung up like phoenix from the ashes — among them the appropriately named "London Pride" reminiscent of the spirit that had survived the onslaught of nights of enemy attention.

There was another war being fought on the other side of the world as British troops advanced through Burma, and American and ANZAC (Australian and New Zealand Army Corps) forces mounted an offensive against the Japanese, but it seemed to attract little attention.

The present peace had been achieved after a struggle lasting six years and there was no reason to suppose that the Far Eastern conflict should be anything but a long hard struggle — the Japanese were known to be tenacious fighters with a reputation for brutality towards their enemies — and victory would not be easily won. But no one was prepared for the news that, on 6th August 1945, American bombers had dropped an atomic bomb on the Japanese city of Hiroshima, followed three days later by a similar attack on the city of Nagasaki. Neither was the world aware of the devastation that saw both cities obliterated from the face of earth, nor of the horrendous loss of life of the population. Outside of scientific circles, little was known of the release of energy by nuclear fission and the world of nuclear physics that had followed upon the splitting of the atom many years before.

It was not surprising that, on 14th August, the Japanese Government sued for peace. The following day went down in history as Victory over Japan Day (VJ Day). The celebrations were jubilant, but the cost in human suffering had yet to be calculated. It was bound to be heavy — the world might be free but at what cost and, more importantly, would it last?

Demob

To say that these events had been totally unexpected would have been an understatement — they were shattering! It took a little time to realize that the ships, planes and guns we had accumulated were surplus to requirement, and a little longer for me to accept that my services might no longer be required. A new word had suddenly entered into my vocabulary — "Demobilisation". Whatever ambitions and hopes I might have nurtured would not now be realized, and whatever feelings I had in resuming my civilian status were tinged with a measure of frustration, knowing that, given the opportunity, I could have made a greater contribution to the success we were still celebrating. But there had been immense benefits that would be long lasting — I had grown up and a few rough edges had been taken off in the process.

Conscription had applied to all. It took young men from their homeland and plunged them into the experience of growing up, and for some it had been a painful experience. We faced the challenge of separation from the family, found the need to make new friends and we had to learn to adjust to the demands of authority without demur. For many the conditions now were better than those at home.

The antithesis of conscription was to be a gradual process with no mad collective rush for the homeward bound train. The logistics of transferring tens of thousands of troops into civilian life were enormous and it had to be done in a just and fair way. It was based on the system of "first in, first out" but with a gradual departure to accommodate the time needed by industry to begin to adjust from the production of armaments to more peaceful commodities.

Once the system got underway, lists of those due for return to "civvy street" were posted in a prominent position in the camp. Their arrival was often greeted with a mixture of euphoria for a few and disappointment for the remainder. It soon became apparent that those with a smaller service number and who had the longer service would head the list, and by a simple comparison I soon estimated that I would, perhaps, have a few more months before my name appeared so that I could join the steady stream of departing souls. In the meantime I would have to find something to occupy my waking hours.

The Government, no doubt mindful of the need to relieve the waiting period, had instituted a scheme whereby service personnel could take advantage of correspondence courses in a variety of subjects, some of which might aid their eventual return to work. I already had a number of City and Guild certificates acquired during my Post Office training, and having some knowledge of the subject I decided to take a short course in Radio with a view of obtaining an advanced certificate. Another of my Radio Mechanic shipmates joined me in this venture, and having completed the course we were given leave to travel to London to take the examination. It had served a useful purpose in keeping us occupied, and the certificate I gained was a useful addition to those I already had.

Demobilisation Centres had been set up throughout the country, and one was directed, at the appropriate time, to exchange a military uniform for a choice of civilian clothing. I had regularly perused the lists, and when my name appeared I was directed to a centre in Guildford in Surrey — why I should be required to travel so far must remain an official secret, but I felt there must be somewhere nearer that could perform this final ritual. By now I was well used to humping my kit from place to place, and I took my leave with hammock, kitbag, case and toolbox for the last time, but not without a tinge of sadness — I was going to miss the comradeship of my shipmates.

In common with many others, I had been offered the opportunity of signing on for another few years in the Navy — but I declined as I had other ambitions and a girlfriend who would not have looked on such a decision with any pleasure. I was required to return my uniform — now well worn — in exchange for a choice of one of two suits, neither of which met with my approval, but having no alternative I selected a non-descript blue woollen outfit and a trilby hat to complete the ensemble. I wanted to retain some memento of my service, and so I removed the badges and buttons from my uniform and kept one of my hammocks in my suitcase — I said that I had lost it and was thereby charged two shillings and sixpence for my felony. My very smart doe-skin uniform was not Naval issue and did not feature in this exchange routine. I still have the badges and buttons, but although my tiddly suit has long since worn out, I have a photograph of both.

The final deed done, I made my way home feeling self-conscious without my uniform but resisting the temptation of saluting the first officer I passed. I felt a sense of pride in having been a Petty Officer in the Senior Service; I would like to have played a greater part, but it was not for want of trying. I was glad to be home and I sensed the relief that Mum and Dad must have felt now that both sons had returned safely.

I had, overnight, become an ex-serviceman and was to enjoy a few weeks leave before being required to return to my former employment as a Post Office Engineer. This gave me the opportunity of visiting my sisters and my brother to introduce them to my girlfriend Joan, and to discuss the situation at home where Dad was making a valiant effort to look after Mum when neither were in robust health. It was clear that I could not continue to stay at home as I would become a burden that was not fair to place upon my father, and it was a family decision that I should stay with my sister in Kent. Since I would be working at Victoria, I was sufficiently close to be able to make regular visits, and with my brother also close at hand the old folk were not neglected.

I did manage a short holiday with Joan to Combe Martin in Devon, but I remember little of the occasion except that the town featured a public house called the "Pack of Cards" — it somewhat stretched the imagination to see that the façade could have resembled a number of playing cards stacked in a triangular formation.

On my return, I sadly took my leave and my memories of the house where I was born. Joan and I married soon after and began our married life in the front room of my sister's house, while my parents departed from the family home to live with my brother in a large house that he had purchased with their welfare in mind. 71, Portnall Road was subsequently sold, but I have remained forever a Paddington Boy!

Epilogue — Progress

Old-fashioned country cottages with old-fashioned cottage gardens and old-fashioned country people to live in them are fast becoming a memory only available to the very old. That bulldozer, Progress, has destroyed them.

The narrow woodland track, the rolling countryside and the quiet country lane is fast giving way to housing estates, factories and roads that are quickly becoming choked with an amazing increase in traffic; the pollution of the London smog being replaced by the even more sinister threat of carbon monoxide poisoning from the exhaust emissions of an ever-growing number of cars and lorries.

Man is undoubtedly cleverer than any other form of creation. In my earliest recollection my daily needs were supplied by a man with a horse and cart, or a young lad struggling with a heavy loaded bicycle. Today I can order what I need on something called the Internet and pay for it by means of a bit of plastic which is capable of containing my life history. I can see pictures of a man walking on the moon, and as I write the world is awaiting a signal from some piece of metalwork that has landed on Mars. If the Scientist would but turn his telescope around and view the scene on Earth around him he would find an infinite number of opportunities to improve the lot of millions on this planet. Man is indeed both genius and fool combined.

But why? Who can tell me the purpose of my short existence on Earth, and why do I enjoy comparative comfort while millions of other races face a lifetime of misery? Many think they may have found an answer in any one of a number of gods in the forms of humans, animals or the sun. Most preach that their god will provide an eternity in some spiritual afterlife, and claim some support from a book that has been amended, translated and made to fit a particular way of life at any given time. Perhaps that is why I owe no allegiance to a Book, a Church or a Creed, but to a Great Spirit of Life and a Natural Law that is evident in all forms of nature. Nevertheless I do subscribe to some form of continued existence, for without it this life would become a mockery of simple justice and contrary to that natural law which dictates that "as you sow, so shall you reap". But, unless it can be produced in a test-tube, the scientist refuses to accept it — he has not yet recognised the existence of a Spiritual dimension to Life.

I had always hoped that I should be able to hand over to the next generation a better world than the one that greeted my arrival some 80 years ago. There has indeed been progress, but has it been for the better? Some time ago I was reading an interesting book by Derek Tangye called "The Evening Gull" in which he

186

addresses the question of progress. It is worth repetition and I am sure he would not have minded my doing so here. He says,

"The price is that FREEDOM becomes choked by more and more laws. One must not flirt with a girl in the office for fear of being charged with sexual harassment. One cannot offer a lift to a woman walking home on a lonely road for fear of being accused of importunism. One must not smoke in public places; one has to obey race relation laws; one must not show affection to a child in case one is accused of child abuse; one cannot advertise for a man for a man's job because one would be guilty of sex discrimination; one cannot choose to put one's own safety at risk by not wearing a seat-belt. And the police, instead of concentrating their financial resources and manpower on real crime, have to deal with these superficial laws, irritating the general public as a consequence, and thereby losing their co-operation in more serious matters as a result.

It seems today's society is unaware that freedom's existence depends on the readiness to take risks. If risks are chained, freedom dies. Legislation is increasingly killing the freedom which men and women in two world wars died fighting to preserve. Freedom means that people can behave foolishly, happily, imaginatively, and yet be ready to be punished if they break the fundamental rules of society. Freedom cannot exist if we are perpetually cosseted by legislation aimed at protecting us from trivial danger.

And where does one learn the fundamental rules that should govern modern society? Where better than at school, and when better than at an early age and still further by the example of our elders? All this before we concern ourselves with league tables purporting to measure the progress of five year olds by some imaginary standard, thought up by some educational egghead. I hope the coming generation will protect those basic standards of behaviour and create a generation where mankind retrieves a sense of balance and realigns his sense of values so that he directs his energies to creating a fair and just world on this planet before seeking to conquer another. He may then become so spiritually evolved that he will realize what an unnecessary and futile exercise it really is."

Appendix —
Intimations of Immortality

The events that gave rise to the above heading began to occur during my early teens while I was still a Paddington Boy, but the effects these had on me went beyond this limited period and were to have a marked influence on my future life. I therefore think that they justify separate consideration.

I had two cousins living in the upper parts of the house who introduced me to a Mr Harry Acres who became a family friend. Harry had a sister who had recently died and with whom he had had a strong brother and sister relationship. Shortly after her death, Harry developed fainting experiences in which, he claimed, he had seen and spoken to his dead sister. As they showed no signs of abating, he sought medical attention and was treated for an epileptic condition. However, the attacks continued.

My sister Dorrie had for some time shown a serious interest in Spiritualism, which it appears was currently favoured by the younger generation, and she suggested that Harry consult a medium with a view to seeking some relief. Soon after the meeting the attacks ceased and Harry began to display some mediumistic qualities in that he could enter into a trance state and, as contact with the medium continued, Harry further developed this ability. Shortly after, séances began to be held in the front room of our cousins' house, to which my sister, my parents and Harry were invited. I went along out of interest and curiosity, taking the position of being seen but not heard.

The proceedings were always opened with a prayer, in order to create a barrier to any unwanted or unforeseen interference. During this time Harry slipped into a trance state. An "entity" spoke through him and identified himself as Peter, who had been a choirboy in his life on Earth and thereupon he sang in the high treble voice of a young boy; he was followed by another being who spoke in a language that no one could understand. Our meetings continued at fairly regular intervals. Harry developed his mediumship, regular speakers put in an "appearance", and "Boy Peter" (as he became known) regularly sang in his high treble voice.

I cannot remember much of what transpired in detail, but sufficient to say that it was worthy of serious and honest enquiry. I knew the people gathered in that room — they were of my own family and incapable of deception, and in any event there seemed little advantage in stooping to such a practice in one's own home. Consequently I joined Doris in her visits to a circle of her friends that met every Sunday in a room above a shop in Westbourne Grove. It was here that I met Mrs Hamilton, who I remember always wore a purple dress on these occasions, and a petite, grey-haired lady named Miss French who was to be the medium for the meeting. The conduct of the meeting followed upon similar lines to those that I had witnessed in our own house and Miss French, who was in a trance state from the beginning, gave a talk along religious or philosophical lines. The talk, in fact, was reputed to have been given by a "spirit guide" who manipulated the medium's vocal chords — in any event I found that the subject did not offend my sense of reasoning.

Other visits followed and my involvement became one of intense interest, although there was much that needed explanation and hence more research during which I maintained an open mind. I continued attending meetings from time to time when I felt so inclined and discovered a common pattern in most of them: the meetings would commence with singing — said to raise the spiritual vibrations — and this was followed by a prayer, often given by the visiting medium who would then give a talk of a religious nature. This would be followed by a phenomenon known as Clairvoyance, a supposed faculty of perceiving things beyond normal sensual contact, or of Clairaudience, a similar faculty involving the hearing. I found the talk to be instructive and in some cases stimulating, but the remainder of the evening by no means convincing, except possibly to those in attendance who were told of the existence of a dead relative in what was known as the Spirit World. There

191

was no attempt at indoctrination; I was encouraged to apply reasoned logic and was advised to put on one side that which I could not accept. My mind went back to the days when I deliberately avoided Sunday School because I could not come to terms with being told that I must believe what my teachers had to say. Those that I met in the Spiritualist movement counselled me to search further and not to accept anything that offended my reasoned logic.

With war imminent, regular meetings were held in the Queen's Hall in London on Sunday evenings. Here a medium named Estelle Roberts went into a trance and, through her "guide", who was apparently known as Red Cloud, gave an address to a packed audience. I attended one of these meetings with my sister, which I remember for an apparent prophecy when the audience was told that there would be fire from the air if there were war. It was not long after that the London blitz saw the arrival of incendiary devices that caused fire havoc all over the City, and the Queen's Hall was a later victim of the bombing.

The ensuing war saw many suffer sudden death and Spiritualist meetings became an attraction, especially for those who had suffered the loss of a loved one. Public meetings were held in the Kingsway Hall in London when Joseph Benjamin and Nora Blackwood were among the visiting mediums. On one occasion I attended, so I can vouch for what I report — I cannot believe that deliberate subterfuge could be employed in the events I witnessed. During the course of the evening both mediums selected individuals from amongst the audience and gave them details of one who had died, in many cases these would be servicemen killed in action in France, young men in the prime of life suddenly catapulted out of one world and into another. It must have been a harrowing experience for those in the audience, and there were some who simply refused to accept such information on the grounds that they had recently heard from the person referred to. As time went on the accuracy of such contacts was checked, and in some cases found to be true and reported in the Spiritualist press. The mediums who attended these meetings and gave their services were all highly respected and proven individuals, and much later I was able to meet some of them and found them to be sincere.

The experience of these meetings reinforced my determination to continue my search for the truth, but my own involvement in the war brought a temporary end to my efforts.

On my occasional periods of leave, I took the opportunity to visit Mrs Hamilton. I remember one occasion when I was in a uniform with black buttons. During the course of the service the medium, Miss French, told me that she could see, clairvoyantly, my buttons being replaced with gold ones. My mind immediately thought of the commissioned ranks that do have gold-buttoned dress, but I had no ambition or intention of joining them; neither did I anticipate any form of promotion in the immediate future.

I did recall that on a previous occasion, before I was conscripted into the Navy, the same lady had said that

I would enter that service but that I would not go to sea. I had hoped for the former, but the latter prediction was, I thought, highly unlikely as there was no likelihood of the war being brought to a close. As for her latest information, I could only wait and see. I kept an open mind as such a subject needed careful investigation, but I thought no more of the event and returned to my Naval duties.

It was some time later that I was summoned before the captain at HMS Nighthawk and interviewed, after which I was told that I had been promoted to the rank of Petty Officer, a position that entitled me to wear gold buttons on my uniform and I proceeded to effect the change forthwith. I record this event simply because it did happen to me and served to strengthen my resolve to carry on my enquiries as soon as I left the Navy.

When I eventually returned to civilian life, I had another hurdle to face — my girlfriend, Joan, was not aware of my interest in "life after death", or in my previous experiences and my wish to continue my enquiries. She and her family were Methodists, and both Joan and her mother sang in the choir at the Tooting Central Hall, in South-west London, a favourite venue for local activities.

I introduced the subject somewhat tentatively not knowing what response I might receive, and I was not surprised when she effectively gave me an ultimatum — the choice was mine. Subsequent events, including our eventual marriage, seem to indicate that I must have succeeded in, somehow, persuading her, as she joined me in my pursuit of knowledge.

194

Joan and I had progressed from the single room in my sister's house and were living in a small flat in Harlesden, close to where I was born. We found a Spiritualist church nearby, which we occasionally visited, and we received an invitation to attend what was known as a "trumpet circle". I had heard of such things before, and feeling this was within the scope of my general enquiries I accepted with eager anticipation of a new experience. There were ten sitters, including Joan and myself, sitting in a semi-circle around a small table on which was standing a cone-shaped object, referred to as a trumpet, that reminded me of a loud hailer often used in the Navy. Behind stood a makeshift cubicle, and when the curtains were drawn the room was in darkness except for a small red bulb, which gave enough light to enable us to see each other.

A lady (the medium) came into the room and took her place in the cubicle, a prayer was said and we settled to await events. In a short time the medium appeared to be entranced and the trumpet rose from the table, seemingly unaided, and circled above our heads before hovering before one of the sitters - I looked closely but could see no signs of the object being manipulated or controlled by human contact.

A voice was heard that seemed to come from the trumpet; this was immediately recognized by the sitter and a short conversation took place. This was repeated to other persons present — there was dialogue on each occasion and recognition of the identity of the voice. After more gyrations around the room the trumpet stopped in front of Joan and a voice, clearly heard, said, "hello Joanie" which she instantly recognized as her deceased grandfather. Further identification followed later when Joan said that her grandfather was the only person ever to have called her by that name. The trumpet then returned to the table and became immobile and the meeting drew to a close - we had both witnessed a demonstration that was dramatic to say the least and which could not be easily explained.

I took the opportunity immediately afterwards of examining the "trumpet" and found it was a lightweight object with no attachments to enable it to be physically manipulated. I decided that this experience needed to be investigated with an open mind, and so I turned to the literature available on the whole subject of Life after Death.

I turned to the Spiritualist Press, a publisher that specialised in the books on the subject, not so much to pick the brains of another but to gain a wider perception and in particular to discover the philosophy that lay behind the physical demonstrations that I had witnessed. Over a long period of time I read a number of books, some of which were mere repetition of the experiences of the author, but interesting as they were they did not advance my search for knowledge to any degree. Others indicated a philosophy that was new to me and seemed to challenge the dogma of the established Church and, what is more, openly invited a critical approach.

In due course I alighted upon a series of books containing the "Teachings of Silver Birch", a so-called spirit guide of what was known as 'Hannen Swaffer's

Home Circle' at which Hannen Swaffer, a well known Fleet Street journalist, held a series of séances with Maurice Barbanell, the founder of a Spiritualist newspaper, as the medium and at which the proceedings were recorded in shorthand. There were six members of his circle, and in addition all sorts of people were invited to hear Silver Birch talk — ministers of all religions, journalists and people from all parts of the world.

The story of how both Swaffer and Barbanell came to be associated in the quest for knowledge is an interesting one, but not the subject of my present deliberations — sufficient to say that the association began in 1924 and lasted many years, producing a number of books which became known as the "Teachings of Silver Birch".

I can do no better than to repeat the comments of A.W. Austen, an editor of one of the books, when he says, "It is not the object of spirit intercourse that we should denude ourselves of the critical faculty and accept blindly the words of another, whether in this world or the next. Nor is it the desire to create a new Orthodoxy, for revelation is progressive and is dependant on our capacity to receive it. The appeal of Silver Birch is to reason, and if anything is not acceptable to the reader's reason it should not be rejected but left as an open question pending further evidence." I found this totally acceptable to my own way of thinking, and his teachings had the hallmark of consistency throughout.

For a long time I had difficulty in accepting Reincarnation or the need for it, but as I deepened my thinking I realized it was an essential part of the evolution of mankind. I concluded that this life has no meaning if, in our short lives, our deeds and misdeeds are not recognized or rewarded in accordance with natural law. Man is indeed, as W.E. Healey tells us in his poem Invicta, master of his fate and captain of his soul.

Further reading introduced me to the Knights Templars of Aquarius and to books written by their founder, Hugh Randall Stevens, who received the contents by means of automatic and inspirational writing, and which confirmed all that I previously understood. I later joined them and met those who had known the author personally and were able to validate the method of communication.

They have all been instrumental in establishing the philosophy on life that I have today. "Our allegiance," says Silver Birch, "is not to a Creed, not to a Book, not to a Church, but to the Great Spirit of Life and His eternal natural laws." As I look around the world today I see strife born of religious intolerance — of Hindu and Moslem confronting each other, of Jew and Arab unable to live peaceably together, and of Catholic and Protestant engaged in a conflict that is over 300 years old. I find in the teaching of all the religious Masters no racial or creedal difference — it is their followers who have amended, altered and translated their word to maintain their individual authority over their flocks.

We are all, irrespective of colour, race or creed, on a pathway of evolution and are at different stages. I find a useful comparison is being given a giant jig-saw puzzle where the ultimate picture is known — before us is a pile of pieces of varied size and shape, and our task in this life, and those lives before and yet to come, is to fashion our own particular canvas. Some pieces are readily fitted into place — those that defy must not be discarded but put on one side until the time comes when their position in life's tapestry becomes clear. But there will be occasions when, in moments of despair, an unseen hand reaches over our shoulder and gently helps us to find a home for just one more piece. Time is not of the essence — and only exists in our troubled world — there is no time to eternity.

As you sow, so shall you reap. As you seek, so shall you find. Much depends on what one sows and what one seeks — the natural laws cannot be ignored or repudiated. In the material life on this Earth there must be, sooner or later, realization of the Spiritual dimension within each one of us. The Kingdom of the Soul is within ourselves and not confined in any majestic edifice or garbed in ornate splendour.

Also available in ISIS Large Print:

Enter Drum and Colours

Alan Brewin

The story of one young man's National service in the 1950's, and how he came to terms with two years compulsory soldiering and the experiences he endured or enjoyed.

From basic infantry training in Yorkshire, to his time spent in Libya and Malta, Alan Brewin details his personal experiences of Army life and the various people he met along the way.

ISBN 0-7531-9992-0 (hb)
ISBN 0-7531-9993-9 (pb)

My Lucky Life

Sam Falle

With great modesty Sir Sam Falle shares his remarkable life in this exhilarating account of life in the Royal Navy and in Her Majesty's Foreign Service

A Jerseyman, Sir Sam Falle joined the Royal Navy and served in World War II. His ship was sunk by the Japanese and he spent three years as a POW. He was later awarded the DSC for "gallantry against overwhelming odds" while serving in HMS Encounter during her last action in the Java Sea. After the war he joined the Foreign Service and embarked on a diplomatic career. Through his choice of career, Sam Falle has often found himself in the most extraordinary and unexpected situations that include being thrown out of Iran; being caught by revolution in Iraq; attending royal visits; backstreet meetings with terrorists and peaceful family days interrupted by distant crises. His memoirs make a most fascinating read.

ISBN 0-7531-9954-8 (hb)
ISBN 0-7531-9955-6 (pb)